P9-DVJ-349

The "I CAN'T BELIEVE THIS HAS NO SUGAR" *Cookbook*

The "I CAN'T BELIEVE THIS HAS NO SUGAR" Cookbook

DEBORAH BUHR

Illustrations by Diana Thewlis

ST. MARTIN'S PRESS   *New York*

THE "I CAN'T BELIEVE THIS HAS NO SUGAR" COOKBOOK. Copyright © 1990 by Deborah Buhr. Illustrations copyright © 1990 by Diana Thewlis. All rights reserved. Printed in the United States of America. No part of this book may be used or reproduced in any manner whatsoever without written permission except in the case of brief quotations embodied in critical articles or reviews. For information, address St. Martin's Press, 175 Fifth Avenue, New York, N.Y. 10010.

Design by Susan Hood

Library of Congress Cataloging-in-Publication Data

Buhr, Deborah.
The "I can't believe this has no sugar" cookbook / Deborah Buhr.
   p.   cm.
ISBN 0-312-04330-9
1. Sugar-free diet—Recipes. I. Title.
RM237.85.B84 1990
641.5'638—dc20   89-78011
                                     CIP

10 9 8 7 6 5

For Tara and Michael

CONTENTS

PREFACE

Good-tasting, allergen-free recipes can be very important to patients and families requiring special diets. Deborah Buhr, who, along with her family, has been faced with a variety of food allergies, knows the importance of being able to prepare foods that look like and taste like "the real thing." Fortunately, Deborah has the ability and patience to develop recipes for herself and her family, and I am very pleased that they will now be available to all people with allergies requiring dietary restrictions. These recipes will help them to avoid the most common food allergens: eggs, milk, wheat, corn, and yeast. The recipes are healthy in other ways as well, in that they contain no sugar, honey, or artificial sweeteners and are very low in cholesterol and salt. With this collection of imaginative breads and desserts, I feel that Deborah has given those on restricted diets some latitude in their food choices and options, presenting a variety of foods that can be eaten even though the basic ingredients are controlled. I highly recommend it to the health-conscious, the diabetic, and those prone to food allergy.

—DAVID L. MORRIS, M.D.
Allergy Associates of La Crosse
Allergy-Immunology
La Crosse, Wisconsin

APPRECIATION

A special thanks to my loving husband, Verne; my two children, Tara and Michael; and to Linda, Kris, Ginny, Marjean, Judy, Cindy, Pat, Rhonda, Ione, Don, Carolyn, Howard, Nancy, Kathy, Janet, Rose, David, Ron, Sue, Ralph, Leona, Renee, Jim, Dr. Morris, and everyone else who helped. Without you, this book could not have been written.

INTRODUCTION

"I can't believe this has no sugar." That's what most people say when they taste these recipes. I take this as a great compliment—and as proof that "healthy" food doesn't have to be tasteless or unattractive looking. It can look just as good as commercial products and taste as good, too.

The recipes in this book were developed for people who have allergies to sugarcane, honey, corn syrup, fructose (which contains large amounts of corn), and dairy products (I have provided alternatives for those people who can have dairy), but they will appeal to other health-conscious people as well because of the following:

- These recipes use all natural ingredients—no preservatives, additives, or artificial sweeteners.
- These prepared foods do not cause the "fast rush" associated with foods made with refined sugar (especially important to diabetics).
- The recipes that call for fruit add beneficial fiber, vitamins, and minerals to the diet (there is no fiber in fruit juice concentrates).
- Most of these recipes are lower in calories than the same recipes prepared with cane sugar.
- Fresh fruit and fruit sweeteners are easy to use and add a wide variety of flavors to cakes, pies, and every type of dessert. Once you become accustomed to the subtle, sweet taste of natural fruit, regular desserts will seem cloying and oversweet by comparison.

It is often the case that only one person in a family has special dietary requirements, making it difficult for the "chief cook" to prepare foods that the whole family can enjoy. This is especially true when it comes to desserts. One part of the family demands the appearance and flavor of traditional cakes and cookies and pies; another part of the family requires something quite different and may feel relegated to a life of plain fruit salad for dessert. Fruit sweeteners are the answer to the entire family's needs.

While taking into account the special needs of the diabetic, the hypoglycemic, the overweight, the allergic, the sugar sensitive, and the health-conscious, these recipes provide the great tastes and textures that the whole family wants. Perhaps more important, they allow the person with dietary restrictions to eat foods that *look like* the foods that "other people" eat. In developing these recipes for my family and friends, the appearance of the final product was just as important as the flavor. If it didn't look just like a comparable commercial product or homemade sugar-based product, I didn't feel any pride in serving it or much joy in consuming it. From experience I know how important it is for a person on a special diet to feel "normal" and to feel as if he's eating the same foods as everyone else. When someone eats one of my desserts and says, "I can't believe this has no sugar," I know he's as surprised by the taste as by how it looks. No cook can receive a better compliment—and I hope it's one you'll hear again and again as you prepare the recipes in this book.

COOKING TIPS AND ADVICE ON INGREDIENTS AND SUBSTITUTIONS

Cooking without sugar is not difficult, but it does require careful measurements, the right ingredients, and a few special techniques. The following sections should help you become a pro in the sugar-free kitchen.

COOKING TIPS FOR SUGAR-FREE BAKING

- Use only *unsweetened* frozen fruit juice concentrates. Make sure these do not contain sugar or corn syrup.
- After years of experimentation, I have found that Minute Maid frozen concentrates work wonderfully. This is because Minute Maid precooks and processes their concentrates in a special way. I have also found that Dole frozen pineapple and pineapple/orange juice concentrates *do not work* in these recipes, and I recommend that you not use them. In my experience, using Dole frozen concentrates in these recipes causes a variety of adverse results, ranging from cakes that deflate to crisps and pies that are runny.

  If you live in an area where Minute Maid pineapple juice and pineapple/ orange juice concentrates are hard to find, ask your grocer if they can be specially ordered; or you may substitute apple juice concentrate in the recipes calling for Minute Maid pineapple juice concentrate. Apple juice concentrate makes a nice-looking product with good texture and flavor, though it may not be quite as sweet. As an added bonus, apple juice concentrate has fewer calories per cup than pineapple juice concentrate.

  The fruit juice concentrates used in these recipes include Minute Maid pineapple; Minute Maid pineapple/orange; Minute Maid reduced-acid orange; Minute Maid grapefruit (which can be used in whole-wheat bread); any brand of grape juice concentrate; and any brand of apple juice concentrate.

- When using frozen fruit juice concentrates, do not thaw; rather, measure out what is needed, adding a little at a time to the egg-and-oil mixture, stirring well before adding more. In this way you will avoid having frozen eggs. The remaining concentrate can then be returned to the freezer in a plastic bag, to be used later.
- When cooking with fruit concentrates, always combine all ingredients well, then stir in baking soda and baking powder quickly, then mix (28 to 30 beats so ingredients are mixed well), *and immediately put the product into the pan and the pan in the oven.* If the baking soda or baking powder is allowed to sit in the fruit mixture, the product won't rise properly.
- If you are allergic to wheat, look for the recipes in this book that call for oat or barley flour. Commercial oat and barley flours are available in most health-food stores (Arrowhead Mills is one brand that I recommend), or you may make your own. To make oat flour, place a quantity of Quick Quaker Oats in a blender and mix on high speed for about two minutes or until oats are very fine. You may occasionally use a teaspoon or knife to push the oat buildup on the sides back to the bottom of the blender. Store leftover flour in a plastic bag. Barley flour can be made in a similar fashion using Quick Quaker Barley (pearled). Another oat flour used in these recipes is Wheat-Free Oat Mix by Ener-G, consisting of oat flour and corn-free baking powder. This is available at health-food stores.
- Measure correctly and you will be pleased with the results. When measuring flour, always tap the top of the measuring cup two or three times with a knife before leveling it off. If a recipe calls for tapping the flour four to five times, this means the flour should be tapped a little more than usual.

    When a liquid measurement calls for a "generous" measure, this means you should fill the measuring utensil to the surface-tension point, that is, to the point where adding more liquid will cause the utensil to overflow. A normal liquid measure would be level with the brim. A "generous" dry measure is a rounded measure; a "scant" dry measure means the measuring utensil will be barely full.
- Freeze or refrigerate food as soon as it has cooled after baking.

INFORMATION ON INGREDIENTS AND SUBSTITUTIONS

- If you're watching your cholesterol intake, you may substitute two egg whites for each whole egg called for in a recipe.
- If you are allergic to corn, be aware that most commercial baking powder

has a corn base. The recipes in this book were created using commercial baking powder. Corn-free baking powder (made with a potato base) is available at most health-food stores (under the brand name Featherweight Baking Powder), or you can make your own with the following recipe:

Homemade Baking Powder

1 teaspoon baking soda
2 teaspoons arrowroot
2 teaspoons cream of tartar

Mix all ingredients well and store in an airtight container.

Yield: 5 teaspoons

Note: If a recipe calls for 1 teaspoon regular baking powder, substitute 1½ to 1¾ teaspoons homemade baking powder.

- If you are allergic to dairy products, try substituting an equal amount of soy milk (available in many supermarkets and most health-food stores) for milk in any recipe in this book. You can make your own soy milk by mixing soy powder (available in most health-food stores under the brand name Soyquick) with water according to the package directions.
- If you are allergic to phenol, an acidic compound used in the lining of many canned goods, use Dole unsweetened pineapple in recipes that call for pineapple slices. Dole does not use phenol in the lining of its cans for pineapple slices in unsweetened juice.
- If you wish to avoid additives and preservatives or sugar and honey, you may want to purchase the following at a health-food store:
    date sugar
    unroasted nuts and seeds
    brown-rice syrup
    unsweetened coconut
    dried figs, dates, and raisins
- There are two types of flaked coconut: sweetened (available in most supermarkets) and unsweetened (available in health-food stores). Sweetened coconut is moist; unsweetened coconut is not. If you want to use unsweetened coconut you will need to add moisture in the following proportion: For every ½ cup unsweetened coconut, add 1½ teaspoons vegetable oil (I recommend cold-pressed safflower or canola oil, but any oil except olive oil will work) and 1½ teaspoons water. Stir well and let sit for 10 minutes until

liquids are absorbed. Use this formula unless directed otherwise in certain recipes. In recipes that call for *dry* coconut, the coconut will absorb moisture from the fruit it's in, so do not premoisten the coconut in these recipes.

- A few recipes call for date sugar, a sweetener made from dehydrated ground dates and that resembles coarse brown sugar but is not refined and contains valuable minerals and fiber. Date sugar adds a special flavor to Chocolate-Date Cake (page 42) and Cinnamon-Spice Bread (page 14). It is available at most health-food stores.
- Use tapioca to thicken fruit puddings, pies, and crisps. It will not affect the taste of the fruit.

HOW TO MAKE YOUR OWN FRUIT JUICE CONCENTRATE

You may wish to make your own fruit juice concentrates for several reasons:

- if you cannot find the recommended products in your area (*however, I would not suggest making your own pineapple juice concentrate!*),
- if you are allergic to pineapple or apple,
- if commercial fruit juice concentrates (pear or grape) contain products that you cannot use,
- if you have mold allergies or other allergies that are aggravated by commercial fruit juice concentrates.

Fruit juice concentrates may be made from either purchased fruit juice (watch labels for additives, etc.) *or* from fresh fruit processed with a juicer. The freshest possible juice is provided by a juicer, of which there are four basic types: the hydraulic press, the centrifugal, the pulp-ejection, and the total juicer. Make sure the juicer is made of noncorroding, acid- and alkali-resistant materials, and follow manufacturer's instructions.

You may make your own fruit juice concentrates from fresh fruit such as apple, pear, and grape (but I don't suggest making your own pineapple juice concentrate).

Place 1 quart (4 cups) fruit juice in a heavy saucepan (so juice will not burn) and heat mixture over medium-high heat until juice comes to a boil. Reduce heat, maintaining a slow boil and stirring occasionally, until the 4 cups fruit juice are reduced to 1 cup fruit juice concentrate. More attention is needed in stirring the mixture as the liquid level is reduced. If the concentrate is reduced to less than one cup, add enough water to bring measurement back to one cup.

Cool fruit juice concentrate, place in an airtight container, and freeze. Substitute homemade fruit juice concentrate for those recommended in the recipes.

Yield: 1 cup fresh fruit juice concentrate

A NOTE ON THE NUTRITIONAL ANALYSIS CHARTS

At the end of each recipe, you will find important nutrition information: the calorie count of each serving; the amount, in grams, of protein, fat, carbohydrate, and sodium; and the diabetic exchanges. The nutritional analysis was performed by Marcia Viers, a registered dietician and certified nutritionist, and is based on the Nutritionist II computer program produced by N-Squared Computing, with input of product nutrient information from various brand-name companies mentioned in the book. The diabetic exchanges were computed by using the Exchange Lists for Meal Planning, a guide developed in 1986 by the American Dietetic Association and the American Diabetic Association.

In using the nutritional analysis charts, you should be aware of the following:

- Nutritional values may vary from brand to brand and will vary depending on the size and ripeness of individual fruits. Thus the nutrient charts in this book should be used as guidelines only, and not as exact measurements.
- Any ingredient listed as "optional" has *not* been calculated into the nutritional breakdown. If you choose to add optional ingredients, be aware that nuts, seeds, and coconut will add substantially to the readings, especially those for calories and fat.
- Whenever two or more choices are given in the ingredient list (for example, "4 egg whites *or* 2 whole eggs"), only the first option has been calculated into the nutritional breakdown. If you use one of the alternate ingredients instead of the first-mentioned ingredient, be aware that the nutritional breakdown of the recipe will change. For example, using whole eggs instead of egg whites will add cholesterol to the recipe; using butter or lard instead of vegetable oil will add more saturated fat and will introduce cholesterol into the recipe.
- Whenever a range of measurement is given for a certain ingredient or whenever a range of serving sizes is given, the first measurement or size is the one used to calculate the nutritional breakdown.
- Only the main recipes, not the variations, have been analyzed.
- The recipes in the final chapter on fresh fruits have not been analyzed. Instead, on pages 138–141, you will find nutritional breakdowns for a wide

variety of fresh fruits, fruit juices, and fruit concentrates. These charts can be used to calculate the nutrients in the various recipes.

- Calorie counts and diabetic exchanges may look high compared to those found in other cookbooks, but portion sizes in this book are quite generous and, we feel, more realistic than those provided in other books.

The
"I CAN'T BELIEVE
THIS HAS NO SUGAR"
Cookbook

QUICK BREADS AND YEAST BREADS

Including Muffins, Pizza Crusts, and Rolls

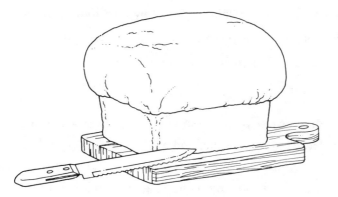

Breads made with natural fruit sweeteners are easy to prepare and can be served at any meal. Slice and toast them for breakfast, spread with sugar-free jam or butter. Try them as the base for your favorite sandwich filling at lunch. Send muffins or individual slices of bread to school with your children or serve them with afternoon tea. At dinnertime, try them with soups, or topped with fresh fruit, pudding, or whipped cream for an elegant dessert.

If you have experience in baking fresh yeast bread from scratch, these sugar-free yeast breads will be a breeze. The mixing, rising, and baking processes are the same as for regular bread, and the "feel" of the dough at each stage will be the same, too. If you are new to bread baking, you'll find that it really is easy. Just be sure to follow the directions closely and to be aware of the feel of the dough.

Realize that the quantity of flour needed to bring the dough to the right consistency depends on many things—the type of flour, the humidity, even the temperature of the air and of your hands—so don't be surprised if you have to use a little more or less flour than called for in a recipe. The important thing is to go by how the dough feels to the touch. Any doubts you have about your abilities as a bread baker will be dispelled by the aroma and taste of your own freshly baked bread. Once you and your family try it, you'll be hooked!

Here are a few hints to get you started:

- Use only the freshest yeast. Fresh yeast will *bubble* when mixed with warm water, fruit concentrate, and a few teaspoons of flour. If your yeast doesn't bubble, throw it out and start with a new batch; otherwise, you may spend the next three hours making bread that won't rise properly.

2

- Measure all ingredients carefully. Add flour gradually until the dough reaches the consistency called for in the recipe.
- When a recipe says to *knead the dough in the pan, do not* take the dough out of the pan and knead it on floured surface. Leave the dough in the pan and add the flour. The recipe will tell you for how long a period you have to add flour and knead. Dough should be soft but not sticky to the touch. For the first rising period, simply cover pan and let dough rise.
- When a recipe says to *knead the dough on a floured surface*, transfer the dough from the pan to a lightly floured surface and knead, adding more flour as needed, for the amount of time indicated. Dough should be soft but not sticky to the touch.
- When a recipe instructs you to knead the dough for one minute after the first rising period and before making a loaf or rolls, take the cover off the pan that the dough was rising in, and knead dough for one minute *in pan. Do not* add flour. What you are doing is moving the fruit sugar around so that the yeast has a new food source.
- Knead fruit-sweetened dough as if it were regular sugar-sweetened dough. When the dough is soft and silky smooth to the touch and not sticky, it is ready for the first rising period. Sometimes the dough will feel rubbery at this stage and the dough will shine. This stage is usually reached after you've been kneading for several minutes without having to add extra flour.
- If a recipe calls for coating the dough with oil, do it gently, with your fingertips.
- Check the dough periodically during the rising period to make sure it doesn't rise too long. With traditional dough, the yeast uses sugar as a food during the rising period. Since you are using natural fruit sugars instead of refined sugar, the yeast will run out of food a little sooner and will start to deflate. To avoid this, set a timer at the start of each rising period and check the dough five to ten minutes before the end of the stated rising time. If the dough looks as though it has doubled in bulk, proceed to punch it down and follow the next step of the recipe's directions.

- As you shape the loaf before the second rising period, treat the dough gently, as though you were working with something fragile, and be sure to roll out the dough to the correct thickness. If you roll out the dough too thinly, it will not make a beautiful loaf; if you are too rough with the dough, the same thing will happen.
- After you put the shaped dough in the baking pan(s), you can determine when it is ready for the oven by its size and appearance. The dough will likely have risen two inches above the sides of the pan, and it will appear to have "little windows" as the gluten is activated and forms strands in the dough. You can see this especially clearly on cinnamon rolls. When the dough reaches this stage, put it in the oven and bake it as soon as possible; otherwise, it may deflate like a pricked balloon.
- If you use your oven as the rising place, remember that it takes seven to ten minutes to get the oven to 350°F, so calculate that time into your rising time and remove the dough from the oven a little before it has risen completely.
- When bread is done, it will be slightly golden on top and will sound hollow when tapped lightly with your fingertips or a knife. When the bread has this hollow sound, remove it from the oven, tap the bread out of the pan (bread will slide out of the pan easily when it's done), and place it on a wire rack to cool.
- Remember that one whole egg or two egg whites may be used interchangeably in these bread recipes.

Blueberry Muffins

1 cup mashed banana
2 egg whites *or* 1 extralarge egg
½ cup water
⅓ cup vegetable oil
2 cups all-purpose flour

1 teaspoon baking soda
2¼ teaspoons baking powder
1 cup fresh or frozen blueberries, left to
  thaw in a strainer

1. Preheat oven to 350°F. Prepare 18 standard-sized muffin cups with paper liners.

2. In a large bowl, stir together banana, egg, water, and oil. Add flour and mix. Stir in baking soda and baking powder quickly, and then mix (28 to 30 beats). Gently fold in blueberries. Immediately spoon batter into prepared muffin cups.

3. Bake about 20 minutes or until a cake tester inserted in the center of one muffin comes out clean. As soon as they are done, remove muffins from tins and cool on a wire rack. Serve warm or cool completely and store in an airtight container in the refrigerator or freezer.

Yield: 18 muffins

PER MUFFIN

Calories: 105
Protein: 2.0 g
Fat: 4.2 g
Carbohydrate: 14.8 g

Sodium: 93 mg
Diabetic exchanges
  Bread: 1
  Fat: ¾

Super-Sweet Blueberry Muffins

1 cup mashed banana
2 egg whites *or* 1 extralarge egg
⅓ cup vegetable oil
½ cup unsweetened pineapple juice
  concentrate (Minute Maid) or
  unsweetened apple juice concentrate
  (any brand)

1 tablespoon water
2 cups all-purpose flour
1 cup fresh or frozen blueberries, left to
  thaw in a strainer
2 teaspoons baking soda

1. Preheat oven to 350°F. Prepare 18 standard-sized muffin cups with paper liners.

2. In a large bowl, stir together banana, egg, oil, concentrate, and water. Add flour and mix. Gently stir in blueberries. Stir in baking soda quickly, and then mix (28 to 30 beats). Immediately spoon batter into prepared muffin cups.

3. Bake about 20 minutes or until a cake tester inserted in the center of one muffin comes out clean. As soon as they are done, remove muffins from tins and cool on a wire rack. Serve warm or cool completely and store in an airtight container in the refrigerator or freezer.

Yield: 18 muffins

PER MUFFIN

Calories: 119
Protein: 2.1 g
Fat: 4.2 g
Carbohydrate: 18.3 g

Sodium: 100.4 mg
Diabetic exchanges
  Bread: 1
  Fat: 1

Cinnamon-Spice Muffins

1½ cups all-purpose flour, tapped lightly 4 or 5 times

½ cup plus 3 tablespoons packed date sugar

Scant 1½ teaspoons cinnamon

3 to 4 dashes nutmeg

Generous ½ cup vegetable oil

⅓ cup plus 1 tablespoon zucchini pulp (puree zucchini in blender or food processor with a little water; drain out liquid with hand strainer)

⅓ cup plus 1 tablespoon unsweetened pineapple juice concentrate (Minute Maid)

Generous 2 tablespoons water

4 egg whites *or* 2 extralarge eggs, beaten

Generous 1½ teaspoons baking soda

1. Preheat oven to 325°F. Prepare 15 standard-sized muffin cups with paper liners.

2. In a large bowl, stir together flour, date sugar, cinnamon, nutmeg, oil, pureed zucchini, and concentrate.

3. Add water and eggs and stir for 2 to 3 minutes by hand. Stir in baking soda quickly, and then mix (28 to 30 beats). Immediately spoon batter into prepared muffin cups.

4. Bake 18 to 20 minutes or until a cake tester inserted in the center of one muffin comes out clean. As soon as they are done, remove muffins from tins and cool on a wire rack. Serve warm or cool completely and store in an airtight container in the refrigerator or freezer.

Yield: 15 muffins

PER MUFFIN

Calories: 152

Protein: 2.5 g

Fat: 7.8 g

Carbohydrate: 17.7 g

Sodium: 98.6 mg

Diabetic exchanges

  Bread: 1

  Fat: 1½

Banana Muffins

Generous ¾ cup mashed banana
4 egg whites *or* 2 extralarge eggs
⅓ cup vegetable oil
½ cup unsweetened pineapple juice concentrate (Minute Maid) or unsweetened apple juice concentrate (any brand)

1 tablespoon plus 1 teaspoon water
2 cups all-purpose flour
¾ teaspoon cinnamon
⅓ cup chopped walnuts
2 teaspoons baking soda

1. Preheat oven to 350°F. Prepare 18 or 19 standard-sized muffin cups with paper liners.

2. In a large bowl, stir together banana, eggs, oil, concentrate, and water. Add flour, cinnamon, and nuts; mix well for 1 to 2 minutes. Stir in baking soda quickly, and then mix (28 to 30 beats). Immediately spoon batter into prepared muffin cups.

3. Bake about 18 minutes or until a cake tester inserted in the center of one muffin comes out clean. As soon as they are done, remove muffins from tins and cool on a wire rack. Serve warm or cool completely and store in an airtight container in the refrigerator or freezer.

Yield: 18 or 19 muffins

PER MUFFIN

Calories: 127
Protein: 2.9 g
Fat: 5.5 g
Carbohydrate: 16.7 g

Sodium: 105.5 mg
Diabetic exchanges
  Bread: 1
  Fat: 2

Banana Bread

Generous ¼ cup mashed banana
⅓ cup vegetable oil
4 egg whites *or* 2 extralarge eggs
½ cup water
2 cups all-purpose flour

Scant ½ teaspoon cinnamon
Scant ½ teaspoon nutmeg
1 cup chopped nuts (optional)
Generous 1 teaspoon baking soda
Generous 2¼ teaspoons baking powder

1. Preheat oven to 325°F. Coat a 9- by 5- by 2¾-inch loaf pan with vegetable oil or vegetable shortening.

2. In a large bowl, and using a hand-operated mechanical beater, whip together banana, oil, eggs, and water.

3. Add flour, cinnamon, nutmeg, and nuts, if desired, to banana mixture; mix. Stir in baking soda and baking powder quickly, and then mix (28 to 30 beats). Immediately pour batter into prepared loaf pan.

4. Bake 50 to 53 minutes or until a knife inserted in the center of the loaf comes out clean. Loosen bread from pan with a knife and turn loaf out onto a wire rack to cool. To store, wrap cooled loaf in plastic and refrigerate or freeze.

Yield: One 9- by 5- by 2¾-inch loaf (12 slices)

PER SLICE

Calories: 143
Protein: 3.1 g
Fat: 6.3 g
Carbohydrate: 18.2 g

Sodium: 147.0 mg
Diabetic exchanges
  Bread: 1¼
  Fat: 1

Super-Sweet Banana Bread

Generous ¾ cup mashed banana
⅓ cup vegetable oil
4 egg whites *or* 2 extralarge eggs
½ cup unsweetened pineapple juice
   concentrate (Minute Maid) or
   unsweetened apple juice concentrate
   (any brand)

1 tablespoon plus 1 teaspoon water
2 cups all-purpose flour
Scant ½ teaspoon cinnamon
Scant ½ teaspoon nutmeg
1 cup chopped nuts
2 teaspoons baking soda

1. Preheat oven to 325°F. Coat a 9- by 5- by 2¾-inch loaf pan with vegetable oil or vegetable shortening.

2. In a large bowl, and using a hand-operated mechanical beater, whip together banana, oil, eggs, concentrate, and water.

3. Add flour, cinnamon, nutmeg, and nuts to banana mixture and mix. Stir in baking soda quickly, and then mix (28 to 30 beats). Immediately pour batter into prepared loaf pan.

4. Bake 50 minutes. Make a "tent" of aluminum foil and place it over the entire loaf pan. Bake another 7 to 8 minutes, or until a knife inserted in the center of the loaf comes out clean. Loosen bread from pan with a knife and turn loaf onto a wire rack to cool. To store, wrap cooled loaf in plastic and refrigerate or freeze.

Yield: One 9- by 5- by 2¾-inch loaf (12 slices)

PER SLICE (USING WALNUTS FOR CHOPPED NUTS)

Calories: 232
Protein: 6.0 g
Fat: 12.1 g
Carbohydrate: 25.8 g

Sodium: 158 mg
Diabetic exchanges
  Bread: 1½
  Fat: 2½

Banana Bread

No Egg

1¼ cups mashed banana
2 tablespoons all-purpose flour
Scant ⅓ cup vegetable oil
¼ cup unsweetened apple juice
  concentrate (any brand)
Generous 2 tablespoons plus 1½
  teaspoons water

2 cups all-purpose flour, tapped lightly
  4 to 5 times
½ teaspoon cinnamon
1 cup chopped pecans
1 teaspoon baking soda
3½ teaspoons baking powder

1. Preheat oven to 325°F. Oil or grease and flour two 8½- by 4½- by 2½-inch loaf pans.

2. In a large bowl, and using a hand-operated mechanical beater, whip together for 40 seconds banana, 2 tablespoons flour, oil, concentrate, and water.

3. Add 2 cups flour, cinnamon, and pecans and beat for 2 minutes by hand.

4. Stir in baking soda and baking powder quickly, and then mix (28 to 30 beats). Immediately pour batter into prepared loaf pans.

5. Bake 45 to 48 minutes or until a knife inserted in center of the loaves comes out clean. Loosen bread from pan with a knife and turn loaves out onto a wire rack, tapping bottom of pan if necessary to release bread. Serve warm or cooled. To store, wrap cooled loaves in plastic and refrigerate or freeze.

Yield: Two 8½- by 4½- by 2½-inch loaves (20 slices)

PER SLICE

Calories: 139
Protein: 2.0 g
Fat: 0.7 mg
Carbohydrate: 16.2 g

Sodium: 100.4 mg
Diabetic exchanges
  Bread: 1
  Fat: 1¼

Banana-Oat Bread

No Egg

2 cups Ener-G brand oat mix (contains
   corn-free baking powder)
1¼ teaspoons baking soda
¼ teaspoon salt

½ teaspoon cinnamon
1 cup mashed banana
¼ cup vegetable oil

1. Preheat oven to 350°F. Coat a 9- by 5- by 2¾-inch loaf pan with vegetable oil.

2. In a large bowl, mix all ingredients quickly so that fruit does not inhibit rising power of baking soda. Pour mixture into prepared loaf pan.

3. Bake 35 to 40 minutes or until a knife inserted in the center of the loaf comes out clean. Loosen bread from pan with a knife and turn loaf out onto a wire rack to cool. To store, wrap cooled loaf in plastic and refrigerate or freeze.

Yield: One 9- by 5- by 2¾-inch loaf (12 slices)

PER SLICE

Calories: 124
Protein: 3.0 g
Fat: 5.5 g
Carbohydrate: 16.7 g

Sodium: 143.4
Diabetic exchanges
  Bread: 1
  Fat: 1

Zucchini-Pineapple Quick Bread

4 egg whites *or* 2 extralarge eggs
Generous ⅓ cup plus 1 teaspoon
   vegetable oil
¾ cup zucchini pulp (puree zucchini in
   blender or food processor with a little
   water; strain out liquid with hand
   strainer)

1¼ cups unsweetened pineapple juice
   concentrate (Minute Maid)
Generous 1½ teaspoons cinnamon
2¾ cups all-purpose flour, tapped
   lightly 4 to 5 times
2⅜ teaspoons baking soda

1. Preheat oven to 325°F. Coat two 9- by 5- by 2¾-inch loaf pans with vegetable oil or vegetable shortening.

2. In a large bowl, and using a hand-operated mechanical beater, whip together for 30 seconds the eggs, oil, pureed zucchini, and concentrate.

3. Add cinnamon and flour to zucchini mixture and beat for 3 minutes by hand. Stir in baking soda quickly, and then mix (28 to 30 beats). Immediately pour batter into prepared loaf pans.

4. Bake 35 to 37 minutes or until a knife inserted in the center of the loaves comes out clean. Loosen bread from pans with a knife and turn loaves out onto a wire rack to cool. To store, wrap cooled loaves in plastic and refrigerate or freeze.

Yield: Two 9- by 5- by 2¾-inch loaves (20 slices)

PER SLICE

Calories: 134
Protein: 2.8 g
Fat: 4 g
Carbohydrate: 21.6 g

Sodium: 73.5 mg
Diabetic exchanges
  Bread: 1¼
  Fat: 1

Cinnamon-Spice Bread

1½ cups all-purpose flour, tapped lightly 4 to 5 times

½ cup plus 3 tablespoons packed date sugar

Scant 1½ teaspoons cinnamon

3 to 4 dashes nutmeg

Generous ½ cup vegetable oil

⅓ cup plus 1 tablespoon zucchini pulp (puree zucchini in blender or food processor with a little water; strain out liquid with hand strainer)

⅓ cup plus 1 tablespoon unsweetened pineapple juice concentrate (Minute Maid)

Generous 2 tablespoons water

4 egg whites *or* 2 extralarge eggs, beaten

Generous 1½ teaspoons baking soda

1. Preheat oven to 325°F. Oil or grease a 9- by 5- by 2¾-inch loaf pan with vegetable oil or vegetable shortening.

2. In a large bowl, stir together flour, date sugar, cinnamon, nutmeg, oil, pureed zucchini, and concentrate.

3. Add water and eggs and stir for 2 to 3 minutes by hand. Stir in baking soda quickly, and then mix (28 to 30 beats). Immediately pour batter into prepared loaf pan.

4. Bake 42 to 45 minutes or until a knife inserted in the center of the loaf comes out clean. Loosen bread from pan with a knife and turn loaf out onto a wire rack to cool. To store, wrap cooled loaf in plastic and refrigerate or freeze.

Yield: One 9- by 5- by 2¾-inch loaf (12 slices)

PER SLICE

Calories: 184
Protein: 3.1 g
Fat: 9.2 g
Carbohydrate: 22.3 g
Sodium: 123.3 mg

Diabetic exchanges
  Bread: 1
  Fat: 2
  Fruit: ½

Waffles

No Egg

¾ cup water

¾ cup plus 2 tablespoons all-purpose
  flour

3 tablespoons vegetable oil

1 tablespoon unsweetened pineapple
  juice concentrate (Minute Maid) or
  unsweetened apple juice concentrate
  (any brand)

¼ cup vegetable oil

1 cup water

1 teaspoon salt

2 cups all-purpose flour

4¼ to 4½ teaspoons baking powder

1. Preheat waffle iron.

2. In a large bowl, stir together ¾ cup water, ¾ cup plus 2 tablespoons flour, and 3 tablespoons oil.

3. Add concentrate, ¼ cup oil, 1 cup water, salt, and flour. Mix well.

4. Stir in baking powder quickly, and then mix (28 to 30 beats). Pour half the batter in preheated waffle iron.

5. Cook waffles to desired doneness. Loosen waffles from iron and place waffles on serving platter. Pour rest of batter into hot waffle iron and cook waffles as before (see *Note*).

Yield: 8 waffles

Note: Extra waffles can be cooled on a wire rack, wrapped in aluminum foil, and stored in the freezer. To reheat, place unwrapped frozen waffle in wide toaster and heat.

PER WAFFLE

Calories: 275

Protein: 4.7 g

Fat: 12.4 g

Carbohydrate: 35.5 g

Sodium: 420.0 mg

Diabetic exchanges

  Bread: 2⅓

  Fat: 2

Stuffing

This is an old family recipe, German in origin, that has been handed down on my husband's side. The original recipe called for 1 to 2 tablespoons of sugar, which I've omitted. Believe me, it's a great stuffing!

Using a nonbasted 11- to 12-pound bird, thaw turkey for three days or so in refrigerator. Remove covering, remove fat and packaged innards, and clean bird, rinsing well with water. Place on a rack in a turkey roaster so the bird does not sit in liquid while it cooks. Season to taste with salt and pepper. Add 2½ cups water to pan.

8 slices bread, laid to dry for 1 day, then cut into 1-inch cubes
4 large apples, peeled, cored, and diced

1 to 1¼ cups raisins
Generous ½ teaspoon cinnamon

1. In a large bowl, combine all ingredients, adding a little water to moisten. (Stuffing should not be mushy—just moist enough to pack your bird. Feel it with your hand; if it packs together, do not add more water.)

2. Stuff bird. Remember that stuffing will expand, so leave a little room. Lace or sew closed turkey.

3. Preheat oven to 450°F.

4. Cover turkey with heavy aluminum foil, sealing edges to keep in moisture. Bake 1 hour at 450°F; turn down oven to 400°F and bake 1 hour; turn down oven to 375°F and bake 1¼ hours; turn down oven to 350°F and bake 45 minutes. During the last 45 minutes, remove aluminum foil from all parts of turkey except legs (and remove foil completely for last 20 minutes of baking time). Baste with turkey dripping every 15 to 20 minutes of last 45 minutes of baking time.

5. Remove turkey from oven. Spoon stuffing from bird and let bird cool 10 minutes before carving. While bird is cooling, add a small amount (about 2 tablespoons) of pan drippings to stuffing. Stir, adding drippings a little at a time until stuffing is just moist. Serve hot.

6. If you have extra stuffing that will not fit into the bird, place it in an oiled glass dish, cover, and bake 45 to 50 minutes at 350°F. When done, add turkey drippings as in step 5 above.

Yield: Enough stuffing for an 11- to 12-pound bird (12 servings)

PER SERVING BEFORE ADDING PAN DRIPPINGS

Calories: 115   *Sodium:* 97.6 g
Protein: 2.4 g   *Diabetic exchanges*
Fat: 0.9 g   *Bread:* ¾
Carbohydrate: 26.5 g   *Fruit:* 1

Baking Powder Biscuits

1¾ cups all-purpose flour, tapped lightly 4 to 5 times
2½ teaspoons baking powder
¾ teaspoon salt
½ cup plus 1 tablespoon plus 1½ teaspoons water
1 tablespoon unsweetened pineapple juice concentrate (Minute Maid) or unsweetened apple juice concentrate (any brand)
Generous 3 tablespoons vegetable oil

1. Preheat oven to 450°F. Lightly oil a small baking sheet.

2. Measure flour, baking powder, and salt into a medium-sized bowl and sift 3 times.

3. In another medium-sized bowl, stir together water, concentrate, and oil.

4. Pour concentrate mixture over dry ingredients, and stir to mix with a fork.

5. Place dough on lightly floured surface and knead ten to fifteen times. Add a little more flour if dough is sticky. Pat out dough to 1-inch thickness.

6. Cut dough with biscuit cutter and place on prepared baking sheet. Bake 10 to 12 minutes or until there is a trace of gold on bottoms, sides, and tops of biscuits. Remove baking sheet from oven and immediately place biscuits in bread basket lined with cloth; cover biscuits to keep them warm. Serve warm or cold. To store, wrap cooled biscuits in plastic and refrigerate.

Yield: 8 biscuits

PER BISCUIT

Calories: 150   *Sodium:* 286.9 mg
Protein: 2.9 g   *Diabetic exchanges*
Fat: 5.5 g   *Bread:* 1½
Carbohydrate: 22.0 g   *Fat:* 1

Soy Milk (or Buttermilk) Biscuits

1½ tablespoons soy powder or dry
  buttermilk (see *Note*)
2 cups all-purpose flour
2¼ teaspoons baking powder
1 teaspoon salt
½ teaspoon baking soda

⅓ cup vegetable shortening or lard
3 tablespoons unsweetened pineapple
  juice concentrate (Minute Maid)
⅓ cup plus 2 tablespoons plus 1
  teaspoon water
Scant 2 teaspoons lemon juice

1. Preheat oven to 425°F.

2. In a medium-sized bowl, combine soy powder (or dry buttermilk), flour, baking powder, salt, and soda. Sift mixture three or four times.

3. Using a pastry cutter, cut shortening into flour mixture until it resembles cornmeal. If you won't be making biscuits immediately, store mixture covered in refrigerator after shortening has been added.

4. Five minutes before you are to put biscuits in oven, in a small bowl combine concentrate, water, and lemon juice. Pour liquid over flour mixture and stir gently just to moisten.

5. Place dough on lightly floured surface and knead gently twenty times. Flatten dough with your hands to ½- to ¾-inch thickness.

6. Cut dough with biscuit cutter and place on ungreased baking sheet. Bake 10 to 12 minutes or until there is a trace of gold on bottoms, sides, and tops of biscuits. Remove baking sheet from oven and immediately place biscuits in bread basket lined with cloth; cover biscuits to keep them warm. Serve warm.

Yield: 10 to 11 biscuits

Note: If not using Soyquick, use cultured Buttermilk Blend by Sa Company and use water instead of lemon juice.

PER BISCUIT

Calories: 165
Protein: 3.1 g
Fat: 7.0 g
Carbohydrate: 22.0 g

Sodium: 312.8 mg
Diabetic exchanges
  Bread: 1½
  Fat: 1½

Cloverleaf Rolls

Knead in Pan

8 cups all-purpose flour

2 packages yeast

2 teaspoons all-purpose flour

½ cup unsweetened pineapple juice
  concentrate (Minute Maid) or apple
  juice concentrate (any brand)

¼ cup water

1¾ cups water, milk, or soy milk

½ cup vegetable shortening or lard

2 teaspoons salt

4 egg whites *or* 2 extralarge eggs, beaten

2 to 3 tablespoons olive oil or oil of
  choice

1. Measure 8 cups flour into large bowl and sift four times.

2. In a small bowl, stir together yeast and 2 teaspoons flour.

3. Place concentrate and ¼ cup water in small saucepan and warm to 120°F. Pour over flour-and-yeast mixture, stir gently to moisten, and let stand for 10 minutes.

4. In a 4-quart or larger saucepan or pot, combine 1¾ cups water (or milk or soy milk), shortening, and salt. Heat mixture to 130°F, remove pan from heat, and let cool to 120°F.

5. Add 2 cups sifted flour to water-and-shortening mixture and stir to count of 20. Add yeast mixture and stir to count of 20. Add 1 cup sifted flour and stir to count of 20. Add eggs and stir to count of 20.

6. Start timing: Knead for 10 minutes in the pan, *not on a floured surface*, gradually adding flour till the dough is soft and not sticky to the touch (you may not need to use all the sifted flour). Make sure you work the dough until it is smooth and elastic. Leave dough in pan, cover with a towel, and let rise in a warm place for 40 to 45 minutes.

7. Generously coat 30 muffin cups with vegetable oil or shortening.

8. Punch down dough, leave *in pan,* and knead for 1 minute. *Do not* add flour.

9. Roll small portions of dough in the palms of your hands to create ninety 1-inch balls. Place 3 balls in each prepared muffin cup. Cover tins with towel and let rise in a warm place for 45 minutes.

10. Preheat oven to 375°F.

11. Bake about 17 minutes or until lightly golden. Remove tins from oven and turn out rolls onto a wire rack to cool. Using a brush, cover tops of rolls with olive oil (or oil of choice). Serve warm or wrap cooled rolls in plastic and refrigerate or freeze.

Yield: 30 muffin-size rolls

Apple-Cinnamon or Pear-Cinnamon Rolls

Knead in Pan

8 cups all-purpose flour

2 packages yeast

2 teaspoons all-purpose flour

¼ cup unsweetened pineapple juice concentrate (Minute Maid) or unsweetened apple juice concentrate (any brand)

½ cup water

1¾ cups water, milk, or soy milk

½ cup vegetable shortening, vegetable oil, or lard

1 teaspoon salt

4 egg whites *or* 2 extralarge eggs, beaten

FILLING

5 tablespoons vegetable shortening, vegetable oil, or lard

1½ to 1¾ teaspoons cinnamon

3¾ cups chopped fruit of choice

1. Measure 8 cups flour into a large bowl and sift four times.

2. In a small bowl, stir together yeast and 2 teaspoons flour.

3. Place concentrate and ½ cup water in a small saucepan; warm to 120°F. Pour over flour-and-yeast mixture, stir gently to moisten, and let stand for 10 minutes.

4. In a 4-quart or larger saucepan or pot, combine 1¾ cups water (or milk or soy milk), shortening, and salt. Heat mixture to 130°F; remove from heat and let cool to 120°F.

5. Add 2 cups of the sifted flour to water-and-shortening mixture and stir to count of 20. Add yeast mixture and stir to count of 20. Add eggs and stir to count of 20. Add 1 cup sifted flour and stir to count of 20.

6. Start timing: Knead for 10 minutes in the pan, *not on a floured surface,* gradually adding flour till the dough is soft and not sticky to the touch (you may not need to use all the sifted flour). Make sure you work the dough until it is smooth and elastic. Leave dough in pan, cover with a towel, and let rise in a warm place for 40 to 45 minutes. While dough is rising, make filling.

7. *To prepare filling:* Place shortening, cinnamon, and chopped fruit in small saucepan and heat until shortening is melted. Remove from heat and cool. Divide filling into three portions.

8. Generously coat three 9- by 9- by 2-inch pans with vegetable oil or vegetable shortening.

9. Punch down dough, leave in pan, and knead for 1 minute. *Do not* add flour. Divide dough into three portions. Roll out each portion on a lightly floured surface to ½-inch thickness. Spread filling on dough. Roll up each portion of dough and filling; cut each into nine 1½-inch pieces (27 pieces total).

10. Place 9 rolls in each pan. Cover pans with towels and let rise in a warm place for 50 minutes.

11. Preheat oven to 350°F.

12. Bake about 25 minutes or until sides and tops are *slightly* golden. Remove pans from oven, turn out rolls onto a plate, cover with another plate, and turn over. Top rolls, while warm, with Apple or Pear Pudding Sauce (page 108) or with butter. Serve warm or cool completely, wrap in plastic, and refrigerate or freeze. Total preparation time is approximately 3½ hours.

Yield: 27 rolls

PER ROLL (USING APPLES AS FRUIT OF CHOICE IN FILLING)

Calories: 198	*Diabetic exchanges*
Protein: 4.4 g	Bread: 1
Fat: 6.4 g	Fat: 1¼
Carbohydrate: 30.3 g	Fruit: 1
Sodium: 81.7 mg	

Pineapple-Cinnamon Rolls

Knead in Pan

8½ cups all-purpose flour
2 packages yeast
2 teaspoons all-purpose flour
½ cup unsweetened pineapple juice
  concentrate (Minute Maid)
½ cup plus 1 tablespoon water
2 cups unsweetened pineapple juice
  concentrate (Minute Maid)

2 tablespoons water
½ cup plus 2½ teaspoons vegetable oil
1 teaspoon salt
4 egg whites *or* 2 extralarge eggs, beaten
Pineapple Topping (see page 23) or
  butter

FILLING

¼ cup plus 1 tablespoon vegetable oil
2¾ teaspoons cinnamon
2 tablespoons all-purpose flour

1 cup plus 2 tablespoons unsweetened
  pineapple juice concentrate (Minute
  Maid)

1. Measure 8½ cups flour into a large bowl and sift four times.

2. In a small bowl, stir together yeast and 2 teaspoons flour.

3. Place ½ cup concentrate and ½ cup plus 1 tablespoon water in a small saucepan and warm to 120°F. Pour over yeast mixture, stir gently to moisten, and let stand for 10 minutes.

4. In a 4-quart or larger saucepan or pot, combine 2 cups concentrate, 2 tablespoons water, oil, and salt. Heat mixture to 130°F, remove from heat, and let cool to 120°F.

5. Add 2 cups sifted flour to water-and-concentrate mixture and stir to count of 20. Add yeast mixture and stir to count of 20. Add eggs and stir to count of 20. Add 1 cup sifted flour and stir to count of 20.

6. Start timing: Knead for 10 minutes in the pan, *not on a floured surface*, gradually adding flour till the dough is soft and not sticky to the touch (you may not need to use all the sifted flour). Make sure you work the dough until it is smooth and elastic. Leave dough in pan, cover with a towel, and let rise in a warm place for 50 to 60 minutes. While dough is rising, make filling.

7. *To prepare filling:* In a small saucepan, stir together all filling ingredients. Bring mixture to a boil, stirring constantly, and simmer until thick (about 2 minutes). Remove pan from heat and cool. Divide filling into two portions.

8. Generously coat two 13- by 9- by 2½-inch pans with vegetable oil or shortening. (You may use three 9- by 9- by 2-inch pans if you wish. You may need another pan, for you will probably have three extra rolls.)

9. Punch down dough, leave *in pan*, and knead for 1 minute. *Do not* add flour. Divide dough into two portions. Roll out each portion on a lightly floured surface to ½-inch thickness. Spread filling on dough. Roll up each portion of dough and filling; cut each into 1½-inch pieces (15 pieces per portion; 30 pieces total).

10. Place rolls into pans. Cover pans with towels and let rise in a warm place for 50 to 55 minutes.

11. Preheat oven to 350°F.

12. Bake about 25 minutes or until sides and tops are *slightly* golden. Remove pans from oven and turn out rolls onto a large baking sheet. Top rolls, while still warm, with Pineapple Topping or butter. Serve warm, or cool completely, wrap in plastic, and refrigerate or freeze. Total preparation time is approximately 3½ hours.

Yield: 30 rolls

PER ROLL

Calories: 202	*Diabetic exchanges*
Protein: 4.2 g	*Bread:* 1
Fat: 6.6 g	*Fat:* 1¼
Carbohydrate: 30.9 g	*Fruit:* 1
Sodium: 76.4 mg	

Pineapple Topping

¼ cup unsweetened pineapple juice concentrate (Minute Maid)
¾ cup water
3 tablespoons arrowroot

¼ teaspoon cinnamon
2 tablespoons chopped pecans
2 tablespoons *dry* coconut

1. Place all ingredients in a large saucepan and cook over medium heat, stirring constantly, until mixture reaches desired thickness for topping. If mixture gets too thick, add 1 tablespoon water and stir well.

2. Remove from heat, beat well, and spread on rolls while they are still warm. To store topping, cover and keep refrigerated, or freeze.

Yield: Enough topping for 30 rolls

PER TOPPING FOR ONE ROLL

Calories: 12   *Sodium:* 0.9 mg
Protein: 0.1 g   *Diabetic exchanges*
Fat: 0.5 g   *Free, or ⅙ of a fruit exchange*
Carbohydrate: 1.9 g

Orange-Cinnamon Rolls

Knead in Pan

8½ cups all-purpose flour
2 packages yeast
2 teaspoons all-purpose flour
¼ cup plus 1 tablespoon unsweetened
  orange juice concentrate (Minute
  Maid Reduced Acid)
½ cup water
½ cup unsweetened orange juice
  concentrate (Minute Maid Reduced
  Acid)

½ cup unsweetened pineapple juice
  concentrate (Minute Maid)
1 cup water
½ cup plus 1 teaspoon vegetable
  shortening, vegetable oil, or lard
1 teaspoon salt
4 egg whites *or* 2 extralarge eggs, beaten
Orange Topping for Orange-Cinnamon
  Rolls (see page 26) or topping of
  choice (optional)

FILLING

¼ cup plus 1 tablespoon vegetable
  shortening, vegetable oil, or lard
2¼ teaspoons cinnamon
1 tablespoon plus 2 teaspoons all-
  purpose flour
½ cup unsweetened pineapple juice
  concentrate (Minute Maid)

½ cup unsweetened orange juice
  concentrate (Minute Maid Reduced
  Acid)
2 tablespoons orange juice

1. Measure 8½ cups flour into a large bowl and sift four times.
2. In a small bowl, stir together yeast and 2 teaspoons flour.
3. Place ¼ cup plus 1 tablespoon orange juice concentrate and ½ cup water in

a small saucepan and warm to 120°F. Pour over flour-and-yeast mixture, stir gently to moisten, and let stand for 10 minutes.

4. In a 4-quart or larger saucepan or pot, combine remaining concentrates, 1 cup water, shortening, and salt. Heat mixture to 130°F, remove from heat, and let cool to 120°F.

5. Add 2 cups sifted flour to water-and-concentrate mixture and stir to count of 20. Add yeast mixture and stir to count of 20. Add eggs and stir to count of 20. Add 1 cup sifted flour and stir to count of 20.

6. Start timing: Knead for 10 minutes in the pan, *not on a floured surface*, gradually adding flour till the dough is soft and not sticky to the touch (you may not need to use all the sifted flour). Make sure you work the dough until it is smooth and elastic. Leave dough in pan, cover with a towel, and let rise in a warm place for 50 minutes. While dough is rising, make filling.

7. *To prepare filling:* In a small saucepan, stir together all filling ingredients. Bring mixture to a boil over medium heat, stirring constantly, and simmer until thick (about 2 minutes). Remove pan from heat and cool. Divide filling into two portions.

8. Generously coat two 13- by 9- by 2½-inch pans with vegetable oil or shortening. (You may use three 9- by 9- by 2-inch pans.)

9. Punch down dough, leave in pan, and knead for 1 minute. *Do not* add flour. Divide dough into two portions. Roll out each portion on a lightly floured surface to ½-inch thickness. Spread filling on dough. Roll up each portion of dough and filling; cut each into 1½-inch pieces (15 pieces per portion; 30 pieces total).

10. Place rolls into pans. Cover pans with towels and let rise in a warm place for 45 to 50 minutes.

11. Preheat oven to 350°F.

12. Bake about 25 minutes or until sides and tops are *slightly* golden. Remove pans from oven and turn out rolls onto a large baking sheet. Top rolls, while still warm, with Orange Topping for Orange-Cinnamon Rolls or with topping of choice, or serve plain, either warm or cold. To store, wrap cooled rolls in plastic, and refrigerate or freeze.

Yield: 30 rolls

PER ROLL

Calories: 215	*Diabetic exchanges*
Protein: 4.6 g	Bread: 1½
Fat: 5.9 g	Fat: 1
Carbohydrate: 35.6 g	Fruit: 1
Sodium: 81.5 mg	

Orange Topping for Orange-Cinnamon Rolls

1½ cups orange juice
2½ tablespoons unsweetened pineapple
  juice concentrate (Minute Maid)

3 tablespoons all-purpose flour
Generous ¼ teaspoon cinnamon

1. Place all ingredients in a medium saucepan and stir until thoroughly mixed. Bring mixture to a boil over medium heat, stirring constantly. Reduce heat and boil gently for 2 minutes, stirring constantly.

2. Remove from heat and cool.

3. When rolls come out of oven and are still warm, beat topping by hand for several seconds and spread on still-warm rolls. To store topping, cover and keep refrigerated, or freeze.

Yield: Enough topping for 30 rolls

PER TOPPING FOR ONE ROLL

Calories: 12
Protein: 0.2 g
Fat: less than 0.1 g
Carbohydrate: 2.7 g

Sodium: 0.5 mg
Diabetic exchanges
  Free, or ⅓ of a fruit exchange

Marjean's Quick Sugarless Yeast Bread

Knead in Pan

6¾ cups all-purpose flour
2 packages yeast
2 teaspoons all-purpose flour
¼ cup plus 1 tablespoon unsweetened
  pineapple juice concentrate (Minute
  Maid) or unsweetened apple juice
  concentrate (any brand)

½ cup water
2 cups water, milk, or soy milk
¼ cup vegetable oil
2 teaspoons salt
1 to 2 tablespoons olive oil or vegetable
  oil of choice

1. Measure 6¾ cups flour into large bowl and sift four times.

2. In a small bowl, stir together yeast and 2 teaspoons flour.

3. Place concentrate and ½ cup water in a small saucepan and warm to 120°F. Pour over flour-and-yeast mixture, stir gently to moisten, and let stand for 10 minutes.

4. In a 4-quart or larger saucepan or pot, combine 2 cups water (or milk or soy milk), ¼ cup oil, and salt. Heat mixture to 130°F, remove pan from heat, and let cool to 120°F.

5. Add 2 cups sifted flour to water-and-oil mixture and stir to count of 20. Add yeast mixture and stir to count of 20. Add 1 cup flour and stir to count of 50.

6. Start timing: Knead for 8 to 10 minutes in the pan, *not on a floured surface*, gradually adding flour till the dough is soft and not sticky to the touch (you may not need to use all the sifted flour). Make sure you work the dough until it is smooth and elastic. Leave dough in pan, cover with a towel, and let rise in a warm place for 35 to 40 minutes.

7. Oil two 9- by 5- by 2¾-inch loaf pans.

8. Place pan with dough on countertop. Uncover and let dough sit for 1 minute. *Do not punch down dough.* Dough will be sticky to the touch.

9. With a little flour on your fingers, cut dough in half with a knife and place on a *lightly* floured surface. (Use the least amount of flour you can get away with.) Gently roll out each half so that it is about 9½ by 6½ by a generous 2½ inches thick. Gently roll up each half, tucking edges under and forming a narrow loaf. Place in prepared pans. Lightly, with fingertips, cover tops of loaves with oil. Cover with light cloth and let rise in a warm place for 35 minutes.

10. Preheat oven to 350°F.

11. Uncover loaves and bake 48 minutes or until bread is golden brown and has a hollow sound when tapped. Remove pans from oven and turn out bread onto a wire rack. Cool for 15 minutes, brush tops with olive oil (or oil of choice), and serve warm or cold. To store, wrap cooled loaves in plastic and refrigerate or freeze.

Yield: Two 9- by 5- by 2¾-inch loaves (24 slices)

PER SLICE

Calories: 158   *Sodium:* 165.0 mg
Protein: 3.8 g   *Diabetic exchanges*
Fat: 3.1 g   *Bread:* 2
Carbohydrate: 27.8 g

WHOLE-WHEAT VARIATION: You may substitute 2 cups whole-wheat flour for 2 cups all-purpose flour in this recipe. If you want, you may use either pineapple or apple juice concentrate, or you may substitute an equal amount of grapefruit juice concentrate if you wish.

Tara's Sugar-Free White Bread

Knead on Floured Surface

7 cups all-purpose flour

2 packages yeast

2 teaspoons all-purpose flour

¼ cup plus 1 tablespoon unsweetened pineapple juice concentrate (Minute Maid) or unsweetened apple juice concentrate (any brand)

½ cup water

2 cups water or soy milk

Generous ¼ cup vegetable oil

2 teaspoons salt

1 to 2 tablespoons olive oil or oil of choice

1. Measure 7 cups flour into large bowl and sift four times. Reserve ½ cup of sifted flour for later kneading.

2. In a small bowl, stir together yeast and 2 teaspoons flour.

3. Place concentrate and ½ cup water in a small saucepan and warm to 120°F. Pour over yeast mixture, stir gently to moisten, and let stand for 10 minutes.

4. In a 4-quart or larger saucepan or pot, combine 2 cups water (or soy milk), generous ¼ cup oil, and salt. Heat mixture to 130°F, remove pan from heat, and let cool to 120°F.

5. Add 2 cups sifted flour to water-and-oil mixture and stir to count of 20. Add yeast mixture and stir to count of 20. Add 1 cup of flour and stir to count of 20. Add rest of flour, 1 cup or less at a time, stirring flour in well before adding more.

6. Turn out dough onto lightly floured surface and knead for 10 minutes. Gradually add more flour if needed. Make sure you work in all flour well. Dough should be soft and not sticky to the touch.

7. Oil the bottom of a large pan and place dough in pan, turning dough to coat all surfaces with oil. Cover and let rise in a warm place for 50 to 55 minutes.

8. Oil two 9- by 5- by 2¾-inch loaf pans.

9. Punch down dough, and knead for 1 minute *in pan*. *Do not add flour*. Cut dough in half. On a *nonfloured* surface, gently roll out each half so that it is about

9 by 6 by 2½ inches thick. Gently turn dough over and roll very softly, maintaining the same measurements, touching it as little as possible. (This will help get rid of any bumps, etc., so bread will have a smooth top.) Gently roll up and form each half into a slender, high loaf. Tuck under edges and place in prepared pans. Lightly, with fingertips, cover tops of loaves with oil. Cover with light cloth and let rise in a warm place for 50 to 55 minutes. After 45 minutes, preheat oven to 350°F. At this time, also check bread so you know how high it is. Dough is ready to bake when it has risen 2 inches above the sides of the pan. When the dough reaches this stage, put it in the oven and bake it as soon as possible. Remember that, since this bread uses only fruit concentrate, the yeast will run out of "food" sooner than if you were using sugar. If you allow the second rising period to go beyond the point at which the yeast runs out of food, your loaf may deflate like a popped balloon.

10. Uncover loaves and bake 50 to 55 minutes or until bread is golden brown and has a hollow sound when tapped. Remove pans from oven and turn out bread onto a wire rack to cool. Cool for 20 to 30 minutes; brush tops with olive oil (or oil of choice). To store, wrap cooled bread in plastic and refrigerate or freeze. Total preparation time is approximately 4 hours.

Yield: Two 9- by 5- by 2¾-inch loaves (24 slices)

PER SLICE

Calories: 158	*Sodium:* 165.0 mg
Protein: 3.8 g	*Diabetic exchanges*
Fat: 3.1 g	*Bread:* 2
Carbohydrate: 27.8 g	

WHOLE-WHEAT VARIATION: You may substitute 2 cups whole-wheat flour and 3 heaping tablespoons wheat germ for 2 cups all-purpose flour in this recipe. If you want, you may use either pineapple or apple juice concentrate, or you may substitute an equal amount of grapefruit juice concentrate if you wish. *Yield:* Two 9- by 5- by 2¾-inch loaves (24 slices)

HAMBURGER-BUN VARIATION: To make hamburger buns, use two lightly oiled baking sheets, and, in step #9, simply divide dough into 24 to 26 pieces and shape into buns. Follow remaining instructions, but bake for only 27 to 30 minutes, or until lightly browned. Cool on rack. Top with olive oil or oil of choice. *Yield:* 24 to 26 buns

Challah (Braided) Bread

Knead on Floured Surface

4 cups all-purpose flour
1 package yeast
1 teaspoon all-purpose flour
2 tablespoons plus 1½ teaspoons
  unsweetened pineapple juice
  concentrate (Minute Maid) or
  unsweetened apple juice concentrate
  (any brand)

⅓ cup water
⅓ cup water, milk, or soy milk
3 tablespoons vegetable oil
¾ teaspoon salt
4 egg whites *or* 2 extralarge eggs, beaten
1 to 2 tablespoons olive oil or vegetable
  oil of choice
½ teaspoon poppy seeds

1. Measure 4 cups flour into large bowl and sift four times. Set aside ¼ cup flour for kneading later.

2. In a small bowl, stir together yeast and 1 teaspoon flour.

3. Place concentrate and ⅓ cup water in a small saucepan and warm to 120°F. Pour over yeast mixture, stir gently to moisten, and let stand for 10 minutes.

4. In a 4-quart saucepan or pot, combine ⅓ cup water (or milk or soy milk), 3 tablespoons oil, and salt. Heat mixture to 130°F, remove pan from heat, and let cool to 120°F.

5. Add ½ cup sifted flour to water-and-oil mixture and stir to count of 20. Add yeast mixture and stir to count of 20. Add eggs and stir to count of 20. Slowly add 3¼ cups sifted flour, stirring well after each addition.

6. Place dough onto lightly floured surface and knead for 10 minutes, gradually adding reserved ¼ cup sifted flour. Dough should be soft and not sticky to the touch.

7. Oil the bottom of a large pan and place dough in pan, turning dough to coat all surfaces with oil. Cover and let rise in a warm place for 50 minutes.

8. Oil or grease a large baking sheet.

9. Punch down dough, knead for 1 minute *in pan. Do not add flour. To make braid (do not add flour):* With a sharp knife, cut off one third of dough and set aside. Cut remaining two-thirds of dough into three equal pieces. Roll each piece into a 13-inch-long rope. Place ropes side by side on prepared baking sheet. Braid the ropes beginning at the center; braid first to one end, then to the other. Pinch ends together to seal.

10. Cut remaining one-third of dough into three equal pieces. Roll each piece into a 14-inch-long rope. Braid as in step #9.

11. Place small braid on top of large braid, tucking ends under. Lightly brush

top of dough with olive oil (or vegetable oil of choice). Sprinkle poppy seeds over dough, pressing lightly to keep seeds in place. Cover with light cloth and let rise in a warm place for 50 minutes. After 45 minutes, preheat oven to 350°F. At this time, check bread so you know how high it is. Dough is ready to bake when it has doubled in bulk. When the dough reaches this stage, put it in the oven and bake it as soon as possible. Remember that, since this bread uses only fruit concentrate, the yeast will run out of "food" sooner than if you were using sugar. If you allow the second rising period to go beyond the point at which the yeast runs out of food, your loaf may deflate like a popped balloon.

12. Uncover loaf and bake 37 to 39 minutes or until golden brown. Remove baking sheet from oven and turn out bread onto a wire rack. Cool for 15 minutes before serving. Serve warm or cool completely before wrapping in plastic and storing in refrigerator or freezer.

Yield: One 13- by 5- by 3½-inch loaf (14 slices)

PER SLICE

Calories: 182	*Sodium:* 121.8 mg
Protein: 4.9 g	*Diabetic exchanges*
Fat: 4.3 g	Bread: 2
Carbohydrate: 30.0 g	Fat: ½

Holiday Fig- or Date-Cinnamon Ring

Knead on Floured Surface
No Egg

6¼ cups all-purpose flour
2 packages yeast
2 teaspoons all-purpose flour
¼ cup plus 1 tablespoon unsweetened
  pineapple juice concentrate (Minute
  Maid)

½ cup water
1¼ cups water
Generous ⅓ cup vegetable oil
¾ teaspoon salt
1 tablespoon olive oil or vegetable oil of
  choice

FILLING

1¼ cups packed, chopped (cut with
  scissors) Calimyrna figs, or dried
  Black Mission figs, or a combination
  of both; or dates (if using dates, you
  will need 32 of them)

½ cup water
1½ teaspoons cinnamon
¾ cup chopped pecans
Generous 1 tablespoon water

1. Measure 6¼ cups flour into large bowl and sift four times. Reserve ¼ cup of sifted flour for later kneading.

2. In a small bowl, stir together yeast and 2 teaspoons flour.

3. Place concentrate and ½ cup water in a small saucepan and warm to 120°F. Pour over yeast mixture, stir gently to moisten, and let stand for 10 minutes.

4. In a 4-quart or larger saucepan or pot, combine 1¼ cups water, generous ⅓ cup oil, and salt. Heat mixture to 130°F, remove pan from heat, and let cool to 120°F.

5. Add a generous 1½ cups sifted flour to water-and-oil mixture and stir to count of 20. Add yeast mixture and stir to count of 20. Add 1 cup flour and stir to count of 20. Add remaining flour, 1 cup or less at a time, stirring flour in well before adding more.

6. Place dough onto lightly floured surface and knead for 8 minutes. Add more flour if necessary, until dough is soft and not sticky to the touch.

7. Oil the bottom of a large pan and place dough in pan, turning dough to coat all surfaces with oil. Cover and let rise in a warm place until doubled in bulk— about 45 to 50 minutes. While dough is rising, make filling.

8. *To prepare filling:* In a small saucepan, stir together figs or dates and ½ cup water. Bring mixture to a boil over medium heat, stirring constantly, and simmer

until thick (about 5 minutes). Remove pan from heat. Stir in cinnamon and pecans and 1 generous tablespoon water. Stir well; set aside to cool.

9. Generously oil or grease a 10- by 4-inch tube pan.

10. Punch down dough, knead for 1 minute *in pan. Do not* add flour while kneading. Place dough on a lightly floured surface. Roll out dough to form a rectangle approximately 15 by 18 inches. Stir filling mixture well and spread evenly over rolled-out dough, leaving a ½-inch border of dough along the long edges.

11. Roll up dough jelly-roll style. Pinch long seam together; join ends and pinch them together to form a ring.

12. Place ring into prepared pan and gently coat dough with oil, using your fingertips. Cover pan with a towel and let rise in a warm place for 35 to 40 minutes.

13. Preheat oven to 350°F.

14. Using scissors, make six V-shaped cuts, each ½ inch deep by 2 inches long by 1 inch wide at the wide end of the V. The narrow end of each V should point outward. Cover pan and wait for oven to reach baking temperature—approximately 5 minutes.

15. Bake for 35 minutes, cover top with aluminum foil (so it won't burn), and continue baking for another 20 to 21 minutes or until top and sides of ring are lightly golden.

16. Remove pan from oven and carefully turn out ring onto wire rack. Turn ring right side up. Cool for 30 minutes and cover with olive oil (or oil of choice). Serve warm, plain, or with topping of choice. This bread makes excellent toast in the morning or can be served cold to dress up any meal. To store, wrap cooled ring in plastic and refrigerate or freeze.

Yield: One 10- by 5½-inch tube loaf (18 slices)

PER SLICE

Calories: 272	*Diabetic exchanges*
Protein: 5.5 g	*Bread:* 1½
Fat: 8.5 g	*Fat:* 1¾
Carbohydrate: 43.9 g	*Fruit:* 1½
Sodium: 85.7 mg	

Banana or Pear Yeast Bread

No Concentrate
Knead on Floured Surface

2 bananas or 2 pears, peeled, cored, and
   sliced
7 cups all-purpose flour
½ cup water (for cooking)
2 packages yeast
1 tablespoon all-purpose flour

½ cup water
1½ cups water
Generous ¼ cup vegetable oil
1½ teaspoons salt
1 to 2 tablespoons olive oil or oil of
   choice

1. In a small saucepan, combine bananas (or pears) and ½ cup water, and bring to a slow boil over medium heat. Cook bananas for ½ hour (pears for 1 hour), adding a little water as needed while fruit is cooking so fruit does not burn. When finished cooking, remove pan from heat, mash fruit, and cool. You will need ¾ cup cooked fruit to use in place of fruit concentrate. When cooked fruit is cool, measure out ¾ cup. Add more water if needed to make ¾ cup of fruit mixture.

2. Measure 7 cups flour into large bowl and sift four times. Reserve ½ cup of sifted flour for later kneading.

3. In a small bowl, stir together yeast and 1 tablespoon flour.

4. Place ½ cup water and ¼ cup of fruit mixture in a small saucepan and warm to 120°F. Pour over yeast mixture, stir gently to moisten, and let stand for 10 minutes.

5. In a 4-quart or larger saucepan or pot, combine 1½ cups water, ½ cup fruit mixture, salt, and oil. Heat mixture to 130°F. Remove pan from heat and let cool to 120°F.

6. Add 2 cups sifted flour to water-and-oil mixture and stir to count of 20. Add yeast mixture and stir to count of 20. Add 1 cup of flour and stir to count of 20. Add rest of flour, 1 cup or less at a time, stirring flour in well before adding more.

7. Turn out dough onto lightly floured surface and knead for 10 minutes. Gradually add more flour if needed. Make sure you work in all flour well. Dough should be soft and not sticky to the touch.

8. Oil the bottom of a large pan and place dough in pan, turning dough to coat all surfaces with oil. Cover and let rise in a warm place for 50 to 55 minutes.

9. Oil two 9- by 5- by 2¾-inch loaf pans.

10. Punch down dough, knead for 1 minute *in pan*. *Do not add flour*. Cut dough in half. On a *nonfloured* surface, gently roll out each half so that it is about 9 by 6 by 2½ inches thick. Gently turn dough over and roll very softly, maintaining the

same measurements, touching it as little as possible. (This will help get rid of any bumps, etc., so bread will have a smooth top.) Gently roll up and form each half into a slender, high loaf. Tuck under edges and place in prepared pans. Lightly, with fingertips, cover tops of loaves with oil. Cover with light cloth and let rise in a warm place for 50 to 55 minutes. (Check bread after 45 minutes so you know how high it is.) Dough is ready to bake when it has risen 2 inches above the sides of the pan. When the dough reaches this stage, put it in the oven and bake it as soon as possible. Remember that, since this bread uses only fruit, the yeast will run out of "food" sooner than if you were using sugar. If you allow the second rising period to go beyond the point at which the yeast runs out of food, your loaf may deflate like a popped balloon.

11. Preheat oven to 350°F.

12. Uncover loaves and bake 50 to 55 minutes or until bread is golden brown and has a hollow sound when tapped. Remove pans from oven and turn out bread onto a wire rack to cool. Cool for 20 to 30 minutes and brush tops with olive oil (or oil of choice). Store cooled loaves in plastic and refrigerate or freeze.

Yield: Two 9- by 5- by 2¾-inch loaves (24 slices)

PER SLICE

Calories: 159	*Diabetic exchanges*
Protein: 3.9 g	Bread: 1
Fat: 3.1 g	Fat: ½
Carbohydate: 28.4 g	Fruit: 1
Sodium: 123.0 mg	

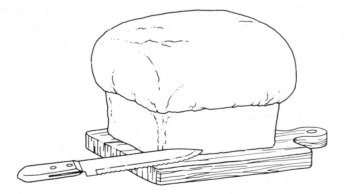

Pizza

CRUST

1 package yeast

3 tablespoons water

1 tablespoon unsweetened pineapple juice concentrate (Minute Maid) or unsweetened apple juice concentrate (any brand)

¼ cup water, milk, or soy milk

¼ cup vegetable shortening or lard

½ teaspoon salt

1½ cups all-purpose flour

Pizza toppings of your choice (tomato sauce, sausage, peppers, onion, cheese, mushrooms, etc.)

1. Place yeast in small bowl.

2. Place 3 tablespoons water and concentrate in small saucepan and warm to 120°F. Pour water and concentrate over yeast and let stand for 10 minutes.

3. In a large saucepan, combine ¼ cup water (or milk or soy milk), shortening, and salt. Heat mixture to 130°F, remove pan from heat, and let cool to 120°F.

4. Add ⅓ cup flour to water mixture and stir. Add yeast and stir. Add remaining flour to make a soft dough.

5. Place dough on lightly floured surface and knead for 5 minutes. Place dough in lightly oiled bowl, turn, cover with towel, and let rise in a warm place for 1 hour.

6. Preheat oven to 425°F.

7. Turn dough onto an oiled or greased 12-inch pizza pan, spread out evenly using your fingers, and add desired toppings.

8. Bake 10 minutes; reduce oven temperature to 400°F and bake 8 minutes more or until bottom of pizza crust is streaked with gold. Remove pan from oven. Serve hot.

Yield: One 12-inch pizza (8 slices)

PER SLICE (*WITHOUT* TOPPINGS; CRUST ONLY)

Calories: 147

Protein: 2.8 g

Fat: 6.4 g

Carbohydrate: 19.1 g

Sodium: 123.7 mg

Diabetic exchanges

  Bread: 1¼

  Fat: 1

CAKES
AND
CUPCAKES

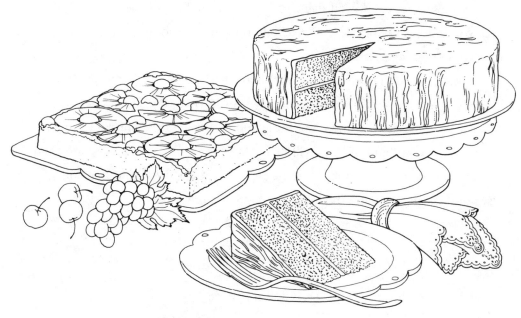

For most people, cakes are an important symbol. They evoke memories of Grandma's kitchen—of mixing bowls and batter-covered spoons. They are an essential part of every birthday and important celebration. And they are the essence of baking—the one item that every cook wants to get "just right" and the item they take most pride in serving.

Most cakes, however, call for refined sugar, so it is with great pride that I present these next recipes, all made only with natural fruit sweeteners. I hope they will bring back the sense of celebration to those who may have thought they could no longer eat cake.

These cakes do not really need toppings; they are great just the way they are! Each cake has a distinct taste and flavor of its own. I've always believed that the cake itself is the important thing and that if the cake doesn't taste good on its own, no amount of icing will help. However, I realize that for guests and for special occasions, you may want to dress up these cakes—and that's fine. Use your imagination and the following hints as your guide.

FROSTING AND ICING HINTS FOR CAKES

Try any of the following as frostings and toppings:

- any commercial whipped topping (please read labels carefully because some contain sugar; corn syrup; caseinate or whey, milk products; or Equal, which contains corn), sprinkled with chopped nuts, moistened coconut, or sliced fruit, if desired;
- sliced fresh fruit such as strawberries, kiwis, ripe peaches, bananas, or dark cherries;

38

- pureed fresh fruit such as blueberries or raspberries;
- any all-fruit jam or jelly (this could be thinned with a little water or fruit juice and heated to make a glaze that is easy to spread over cooled cake);
- whipped cream cheese, with or without nuts (especially good on Deluxe Carrot Cake, page 50);
- plain yogurt, topped with sliced fresh fruit or chopped nuts, if desired.

LAYER CAKES

The following cakes can be turned into layer cakes simply by switching from one type of baking pan to another. (For information on turning the cake batter into layers, see the instructions at the end of each recipe. Apply the frosting of your choice between layers and on top.)

- Chocolate-Date Cake (page 42)
- Chocolate-Coconut Cake (page 44)
- Milk Chocolate Cake (page 45)
- Carrot Sunshine Cake (page 49)
- Deluxe Carrot Cake (page 50)
- Orange–Poppy Seed Cake (page 52)
- Pineapple-Cherry Upside-Down Cake (batter only; page 56)

CUPCAKES

Cupcakes are a special treat for kids and make wonderful lunch-box desserts. These five cake recipes will make excellent cupcakes:

- Chocolate-Date Cake (page 42)
- Carrot Sunshine Cake (page 49)
- Deluxe Carrot Cake (page 50)

- Orange–Poppy Seed Cake made using straight apple juice concentrate (page 52)
- Pineapple-Cherry Upside-Down Cake (batter only; page 56)

For information on turning the cake batter into cupcakes, see the instructions at the end of each recipe.

SUBSTITUTIONS

Remember that 1 whole egg is interchangeable with every 2 egg whites used in these cake recipes.

Carob powder and cocoa powder are also interchangeable in these recipes, but you should be aware that most brands of carob contain milk and most brands of cocoa contain cornstarch. Read labels and call the companies if you are in doubt and have allergies. For milk-free recipes, use cocoa; for corn-free recipes, use carob. For milk-free, corn-free recipes, use chocolate. For each 3 tablespoons of carob or cocoa powder, use 1 square of chocolate and decrease the milk, water, or other liquid in the recipe by 1 tablespoon. (*Note:* A spokesperson for the Hershey Chocolate Company has stated that Hershey adds neither corn nor dairy products to its cocoa. A spokesperson for General Foods Corporation has stated that the company adds neither corn nor dairy products to its Baker's All-Natural Unsweetened Chocolate.)

Nutty No-Sugar Brownies

½ cup plus 3 tablespoons vegetable oil
1½ cups date sugar, tapped well
½ cup minus 1½ teaspoons water
6 egg whites *or* 3 extralarge eggs
¾ cup all-purpose flour
½ cup well-packed unsweetened cocoa
  powder or unsweetened carob
  powder (see page 40)

½ teaspoon salt
½ cup chopped nuts
¾ teaspoon baking soda

1. Preheat oven to 350°F. Oil the bottom only of a 9- by 9- by 2-inch baking pan.

2. In a large bowl, stir together all ingredients except baking soda until well combined. Stir in baking soda quickly, and then mix (28 to 30 beats); immediately pour mixture into prepared baking pan.

3. Bake 20 minutes at 350°F. Turn down oven to 325°F and bake another 15 minutes or until a cake tester inserted in center of brownies comes out clean.

4. Remove pan from oven and place on a wire rack. Cool 30 minutes before cutting brownies, with a knife, into squares for serving. To store, place cooled brownies in an airtight container and refrigerate or freeze.

Yield: 9 servings

PER SERVING (USING WALNUTS FOR CHOPPED NUTS)

Calories: 315
Protein: 6.3 g
Fat: 21.7 g
Carbohydrate: 27.0 g

Sodium: 70.3 mg
Diabetic exchanges
  Bread: 1¼
  Fat: 4¼

Chocolate-Date Cake

No Eggs

1¾ cups all-purpose flour, tapped lightly 4 to 5 times
1 cup packed date sugar
¼ cup plus 1 tablespoon unsweetened cocoa powder or unsweetened carob powder (see page 40)
½ teaspoon salt
⅓ cup vegetable oil
¼ cup unsweetened grape juice concentrate (any brand)
¼ cup unsweetened pineapple juice concentrate (Minute Maid)
1 cup plus 3 tablespoons plus 2 teaspoons water
1½ teaspoons baking soda
Chocolate-Date Frosting (see page 43)

1. Preheat oven to 325°F. Oil a 9- by 9- by 2-inch baking pan.

2. In a large bowl, and using a fork, stir together flour, date sugar, cocoa, and salt. Set aside.

3. In a medium-sized bowl, combine oil, concentrates, and water. Beat mixture for 30 seconds with a hand-operated mechanical beater. Add concentrate mixture to flour mixture and beat well, by hand, for 4 minutes. Stir in baking soda quickly, and then mix (28 to 30 beats); immediately pour mixture into prepared baking pan.

4. Bake 40 minutes or until a cake tester inserted in center of cake comes out clean.

5. Remove pan from oven and place on a wire rack until cake is completely cooled. Frost with Chocolate-Date Frosting. To store, place frosted cake in airtight container and refrigerate or freeze.

Yield: One 9- by 9- by 2-inch cake (9 servings)

PER SERVING

Calories: 240
Protein: 3.7 g
Fat: 8.8 g
Carbohydrate: 37.8 g
Sodium: 251.7 mg

Diabetic exchanges
  Bread: 1
  Fat: 1¾
  Fruit: 1½

CUPCAKE VARIATION: This Chocolate-Date Cake is very moist and therefore makes excellent cupcakes. Follow the same instructions as for the cake, but use 16 or 17 muffin cups (with paper liners) and reduce the baking time to 17 to 19 minutes (at 325°F). Use a cake tester to test for doneness. When done, remove tins from oven and remove cupcakes to a table or wire rack to cool. Frost with Chocolate-Date Frosting.

LAYER-CAKE VARIATIONS: For an 8½-inch round layer cake, simply pour batter into two generously oiled or greased (or grease bottom and sides of pans and place waxed paper on pan bottoms) 8½-inch round cake pans. Bake 24 to 26 minutes at 325°F. Use a cake tester to test for doneness. Remove pans from oven and place on a wire rack. Cool 10 minutes before loosening cake from sides of pan with a knife and removing cake from pan. To frost the center, top, and sides of cake, double the recipe for Chocolate-Date Frosting.

For a 9-inch round layer cake, simply pour batter into two generously oiled or greased (or grease bottom and sides of pans and place waxed paper on pan bottoms) 9-inch round cake pans. Bake 22 to 24 minutes at 325°F. Use a cake tester to test for doneness. Follow rest of instructions given in preceding 8½-inch Layer-Cake Variation.

Chocolate-Date Frosting

1 ounce (1 square) Baker's All-Natural Unsweetened Chocolate	5 tablespoons water
1 tablespoon vegetable oil	½ cup date sugar

1. In a small saucepan, melt chocolate, oil, and water over medium heat.

2. Reduce heat to low, add date sugar, and cook, stirring, for 2 to 2½ minutes.

3. Remove pan from heat and continue to stir mixture for 1 to 2 minutes. Spread frosting on cooled cake.

Yield: Enough frosting for one 9- by 9- by 2-inch cake, or 16 or 17 cupcakes (9 servings). Double recipe to frost center, top, and sides of a layer cake.

PER SERVING

Calories: 51	*Sodium:* 0.1 mg
Protein: 0.6 g	*Diabetic exchanges*
Fat: 3.1 g	*Fat:* ⅔
Carbohydrate: 6.2 g	*Fruit:* ⅓

Chocolate-Coconut Cake

6 egg whites *or* 3 extralarge eggs

¾ cup vegetable oil

1 cup unsweetened pineapple juice concentrate (Minute Maid)

1 cup unsweetened grape juice concentrate (any brand)

1 tablespoon plus 1½ teaspoons soy powder or 3 tablespoons plus 2½ teaspoons dry milk powder or 1 tablespoon plus 1½ teaspoons all-purpose flour

2 cups plus 2 tablespoons plus 1½ teaspoons all-purpose flour, tapped lightly 4 or 5 times

½ cup firmly packed unsweetened cocoa powder or unsweetened carob powder (see page 40)

¾ cup unsweetened coconut, premoistened with 2 teaspoons water and 2 teaspoons vegetable oil

2 teaspoons baking soda

1. Preheat oven to 350°F. Oil and flour a 13- by 9- by 2-inch baking pan.

2. In a large bowl, combine eggs, oil, concentrates, and soy powder (or dry milk or flour). Beat mixture for 30 seconds with a hand-operated mechanical beater. Add flour, cocoa, and coconut and beat well. Stir in baking soda quickly and then mix (28 to 30 beats); immediately pour mixture into prepared baking pan.

3. Bake 25 minutes at 350°F. Turn down oven to 325°F and bake another 8 to 10 minutes or until a cake tester inserted in center of cake comes out clean.

4. Remove pan from oven and place on a wire rack until cake is completely cooled. To store, place cooled cake in an airtight container and refrigerate or freeze.

Yield: One 13- by 9- by 2-inch cake (15 servings)

PER SERVING

Calories: 359

Protein: 7.0 g

Fat: 14.0 g

Carbohydrate: 52.2 g

Sodium: 145.2 mg

Diabetic exchanges

  Bread: 2

  Fat: 2¾

  Fruit: 1½

LAYER-CAKE VARIATION: For a 9-inch round layer cake, pour batter into two generously oiled or greased and floured (or grease bottom and sides of pans and place waxed paper on pan bottoms) 9-inch round cake pans. Bake at 350°F for 25 minutes. Turn oven down to 325°F and bake for 6 minutes more or until a cake tester inserted in center of cake comes out clean. Remove pans from oven and place on a wire rack. Cool 10 minutes before loosening cake from sides of pans with a knife and removing cake from pans. Apply frosting of your choice between layers and on top.

Milk Chocolate Cake

2 cups frozen, dark, sweet cherries

2 to 4 tablespoons water

4 egg whites *or* 2 extralarge eggs

⅓ cup vegetable oil

¼ cup unsweetened grape juice concentrate (any brand)

¼ cup unsweetened pineapple juice concentrate (Minute Maid)

1 tablespoon plus 2 teaspoons soy powder *or* 4 tablespoons dry milk powder *or* 1 tablespoon plus 2 teaspoons all-purpose flour

1⅓ cups all-purpose flour, tapped lightly 4 to 5 times

¼ cup firmly packed unsweetened cocoa powder or unsweetened carob powder (see page 40)

1¼ teaspoons baking soda

1. Preheat oven to 325°F. Oil and flour a 9- by 9- by 2-inch baking pan.

2. Puree frozen cherries and water in a blender. Blend till mixture turns and folds when blender is on. Place puree in a small strainer over a small bowl and let drain for 10 minutes, stirring occasionally. Pour pulp remaining in strainer into a measuring cup and add enough of the juice to make ¾ cup of pulp and juice.

3. In a large bowl, combine ¾ cup cherry pulp and juice, eggs, oil, concentrates, and soy powder (or dry milk or flour). Beat mixture for 30 seconds with a hand-operated mechanical beater. Add 1⅓ cups flour and cocoa; beat well. Stir in baking soda quickly, and then mix (28 to 30 beats); immediately pour mixture into prepared baking pan.

4. Bake about 31 minutes or until a cake tester inserted in center of cake comes out clean.

5. Remove pan from oven and place on a wire rack until cake is completely cooled. To store, place cooled cake in an airtight container and refrigerate or freeze.

Yield: One 9- by 9- by 2-inch cake (9 servings)

PER SERVING OF MILK CHOCOLATE CAKE

Calories: 209	*Diabetic exchanges*
Protein: 4.7 g	*Bread:* 1¼
Fat: 9.1 g	*Fat:* 1¾
Carbohydrate: 28.2 g	*Fruit:* ½
Sodium: 142.6 mg	

MILK CHOCOLATE LAYER-CAKE VARIATIONS: For an 8½-inch round layer cake, sim-ply pour batter into two generously oiled or greased and floured (or grease bottom and sides of pans and place waxed paper on pan bottoms) 8½-inch round cake pans. Bake at 325°F for 21 to 23 minutes, or until a cake tester inserted in center of cake comes out clean. Remove pans from oven and place on a wire rack. Cool 10 minutes before loosening cake from sides of pans with a knife and removing cakes from pans. Apply frosting of your choice between layers and on top.

For an 8½-inch round four-layer cake, just double the batter and use four 8½-inch round layer cake pans.

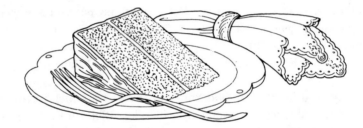

Banana-Pecan Cake

TOPPING

¼ cup chopped pecans
¼ teaspoon cinnamon

CAKE

¾ cup mashed banana
⅓ cup vegetable oil
6 egg whites *or* 3 extralarge eggs
1 cup unsweetened pineapple juice
  concentrate (Minute Maid)
¼ cup unsweetened orange juice
  concentrate (Minute Maid Reduced
  Acid)

1½ teaspoons cinnamon
2¼ cups all-purpose flour
½ cup chopped pecans
2 teaspoons baking soda

1. Preheat oven to 325°F. Oil and flour a 13- by 9- by 2-inch baking pan.

2. *To make topping:* In a small bowl, stir together pecans and cinnamon with a fork and set aside.

3. In a large bowl, combine banana, oil, eggs, and concentrates. Beat mixture for 1 minute with a hand-operated mechanical beater. Add cinnamon and flour and beat well by hand. Add ½ cup pecans and stir for 1 to 2 minutes. Stir in baking soda quickly, and then mix (28 to 30 beats); immediately spoon batter into prepared baking pan. Sprinkle pecan topping evenly over mixture.

4. Bake about 32 minutes or until a cake tester inserted in center of cake comes out clean.

5. Remove pan from oven and place on a wire rack until cake is completely cooled. To store, place cooled cake in an airtight container and refrigerate or freeze.

Yield: One 13- by 9- by 2-inch cake (15 servings)

PER SERVING WITH TOPPING

Calories: 210
Protein: 4.1 g
Fat: 9.0 g
Carbohydrate: 28.7 g
Sodium: 138.4 mg

Diabetic exchanges
  Bread: 1
  Fat: 1¾
  Fruit: ¼

Lemon Cake

TOPPING

¾ cup *dry* unsweetened coconut (if leaving out fruit in topping, premoisten coconut with 2¼ teaspoons water and 2¼ teaspoons oil)

½ cup chopped and drained (*not packed*) pineapple (optional; press lightly with spoon in hand strainer to reduce moisture content)

⅓ cup peeled, chopped, and drained (*not packed*) orange (optional; press lightly with spoon in hand strainer to reduce moisture content)

¼ teaspoon cinnamon

¼ cup sesame seeds

½ cup chopped nuts

½ cup unsweetened coconut, premoistened with 1½ teaspoons water and 1½ teaspoons vegetable oil (used to sprinkle over topping)

CAKE

8 egg whites *or* 4 extralarge eggs

½ cup vegetable oil

1 tablespoon water

One 6-ounce can unsweetened pineapple/orange juice concentrate (Minute Maid)

⅓ cup lemon juice

Generous 2 cups all-purpose flour

¼ teaspoon cinnamon

3 dashes nutmeg

1 teaspoon baking soda

2½ teaspoons baking powder

1. Preheat oven to 350°F. Oil and flour a 13- by 9- by 2-inch baking pan.

2. *To make topping:* In a medium-sized bowl and using a fork, stir together all topping ingredients except the ½ cup premoistened coconut. Set aside.

3. In a large bowl, combine eggs, oil, water, concentrate, and lemon juice and beat by hand for 30 seconds. Add flour, cinnamon, and nutmeg; stir well. Stir in baking soda and baking powder quickly, and then mix (28 to 30 beats); immediately pour mixture into prepared baking pan. Spoon moist topping over cake. Sprinkle ½ cup premoistened coconut over entire cake.

4. Bake 30 minutes or until a cake tester inserted in center of cake comes out clean.

5. Remove pan from oven and place on a wire rack until cake is completely cooled. To store, place cooled cake in an airtight container and refrigerate or freeze.

Yield: One 13- by 9- by 2-inch cake (15 servings)

PER SERVING WITH TOPPING

Calories: 229
Protein: 4.5 g
Fat: 14.2 g
Carbohydrate: 21.3 g
Sodium: 144.6 mg

Diabetic exchanges
  Bread: 1
  Fat: 2¾
  Fruit: ½

Carrot Sunshine Cake

6 egg whites *or* 3 extralarge eggs
½ cup vegetable oil
1 cup unsweetened pineapple juice
  concentrate (Minute Maid)
¼ cup unsweetened orange juice
  concentrate (Minute Maid Reduced
  Acid)

2 teaspoons cinnamon
1 cup packed grated carrot
Scant 2½ cups all-purpose flour
2½ teaspoons baking soda

1. Preheat oven to 325°F. Oil and flour a 13- by 9- by 2-inch baking pan.
2. In a large bowl, combine eggs, oil, and concentrates. Using a hand-operated mechanical beater, beat mixture until foamy—about 1 minute. Add cinnamon, carrot, and flour; beat by hand for 2 to 3 minutes. Stir in baking soda quickly, and then mix (28 to 30 beats); immediately pour mixture into prepared baking pan.
3. Bake 30 minutes or until a cake tester inserted in center of cake comes out clean.
4. Remove pan from oven and place on a wire rack until cake is completely cooled. To store, place cooled cake in an airtight container and refrigerate or freeze.

Yield: One 13- by 9- by 2-inch cake (15 servings)

PER SERVING

Calories: 189
Protein: 3.8 g
Fat: 0.4 g
Carbohydrate: 27.4 g
Sodium: 168.2 mg

Diabetic exchanges
  Bread: 1
  Fat: 1½
  Fruit: ¾

CARROT SUNSHINE CUPCAKE VARIATION: This carrot cake makes excellent cupcakes. Follow the same instructions as for the cake, but use 30 muffin cups with paper liners and reduce the baking time to 17 to 19 minutes (at 325°F). Use a cake tester to test for doneness. When done, remove tins from the oven and remove cupcakes to a table or wire rack to cool.

CARROT SUNSHINE LAYER-CAKE VARIATION: For a 9-inch round layer cake, pour batter into two generously oiled or greased and floured (or grease bottom and sides of pans and place waxed paper on pan bottoms) 9-inch round cake pans. Bake at 325°F for 22 to 25 minutes or until a cake tester inserted in center of cake comes out clean. Remove pans from oven and place on a wire rack. Cool 10 minutes before loosening cake from sides of pans with a knife and removing cake from pans. Apply frosting of your choice between layers and on top.

Deluxe Carrot Cake

6 egg whites *or* 3 extralarge eggs
½ cup vegetable oil
1 cup unsweetened pineapple juice concentrate (Minute Maid)
¼ cup unsweetened orange juice concentrate (Minute Maid Reduced Acid)

2¼ teaspoons cinnamon
1½ cups packed grated carrot
2½ cups all-purpose flour, tapped lightly 4 to 5 times
2½ teaspoons baking soda

1. Preheat oven to 325°F. Oil and flour a 13- by 9- by 2-inch baking pan.

2. In a large bowl, combine eggs, oil, and concentrates. Using a hand-operated mechanical beater, beat mixture until foamy—about 1 minute. Add cinnamon, carrot, and flour; beat by hand for 2 minutes. Stir in baking soda quickly, and then mix (28 to 30 beats); immediately pour mixture into prepared baking pan.

3. Bake 33 to 35 minutes or until a cake tester inserted in center of cake comes out clean.

4. Remove pan from oven and place on a wire rack until cake is completely cooled. To store, place cooled cake in an airtight container and refrigerate or freeze.

Yield: One 13- by 9- by 2-inch cake (15 servings)

PER SERVING

Calories: 191   *Diabetic exchanges*
Protein: 3.9 g   *Bread:* 1
Fat: 7.4 g   *Fat:* 1½
Carbohydrate: 27.8 g   *Fruit:* ¼
Sodium: 169.5 mg

CUPCAKE VARIATION: This carrot cake is very moist and therefore makes excellent cupcakes. Follow the same instructions as for the cake, but use 30 muffin cups with paper liners and reduce the baking time to 19 to 20 minutes (at 325°F). Use a cake tester to test for doneness. When done, remove tins from oven and remove cupcakes to a table or wire rack to cool.

LAYER-CAKE VARIATION: For a 9-inch round layer cake, pour batter into two generously oiled or greased and floured (or grease bottom and sides of pans and place waxed paper on pan bottoms) 9-inch round cake pans. Bake at 325°F for 25 to 28 minutes or until a cake tester inserted in center of cake comes out clean. Remove pans from oven and place on a wire rack. Cool 10 minutes before loosening cake from sides of pans with a knife and removing cake from pans. Apply frosting of your choice between layers and on top.

Orange–Poppy Seed Cake

By changing the amount and kinds of concentrates, this cake can be made four different ways, each with its own wonderful flavor (see Apple and Pineapple Variations).

8 egg whites *or* 4 extralarge eggs
½ cup vegetable oil
1¼ cups unsweetened pineapple juice concentrate (Minute Maid)
¾ cup plus 1 tablespoon unsweetened orange juice concentrate (Minute Maid Reduced Acid)

1 tablespoon plus 2 teaspoons poppy seeds (optional)
1½ teaspoons cinnamon
2¾ cups all-purpose flour
2½ teaspoons baking soda

1. Preheat oven to 325°F. Oil and flour a 13- by 9- by 2-inch baking pan. Also fill two cups of a standard-sized muffin tin with paper liners because this recipe makes just a little too much batter for this size pan.

2. In a large bowl, combine eggs, oil, pineapple and orange concentrates, 1 tablespoon poppy seeds, and cinnamon. Beat for 1 minute with a hand-operated mechanical beater. Add flour and beat well by hand for 2 minutes. Stir in baking soda quickly, and then mix (28 to 30 beats); immediately pour mixture into prepared baking pan and two muffin cups. Sprinkle remaining poppy seeds on top.

3. Place cupcakes and cake in oven at the same time. Bake cupcakes for 20 minutes or until a cake tester inserted in center comes out clean. Remove tin from oven and remove cupcakes to a wire rack to cool. Reset timer and bake cake 10 minutes longer. Reduce heat to 300°F and continue baking for another 10 minutes or until a cake tester inserted in center of cake comes out clean.

4. Remove pan from oven and place on a wire rack until cake is completely cooled. To store, place cooled cake in an airtight container and refrigerate or freeze.

Yield: One 13- by 9- by 2-inch cake plus 2 cupcakes (17 servings)

PER SERVING

Calories: 199
Protein: 4.2 g
Fat: 6.6 g
Carbohydrate: 30.6 g
Sodium: 156.9 mg

Diabetic exchanges
  Bread: 1¼
  Fat: ¾
  Fruit: 1¼

APPLE AND PINEAPPLE VARIATIONS: For more of an original poppy seed–cake flavor, use only unsweetened pineapple juice concentrate—that is, 2 cups plus 1 tablespoon.

For a light apple-orange flavor, substitute 1¼ cups unsweetened apple juice concentrate and ¾ cup plus 1 tablespoon unsweetened orange juice concentrate for the pineapple and orange juice concentrates.

For a mild apple flavor, substitute 2 cups plus 1 tablespoon unsweetened apple juice concentrate for the pineapple and orange juice concentrates.

CUPCAKE VARIATION: If you wish to make cupcakes, I would suggest using only unsweetened apple juice concentrate. This will make the cupcakes moist, with good texture and flavor. The other concentrates seem to produce a dryer product.

Follow the same instructions as for the cake, but substitute an equal amount of apple juice concentrate for both the pineapple and orange juice concentrates—that is, 2 cups plus 1 tablespoon.

Fill thirty muffin cups with paper liners and reduce the baking time to 19 to 20 minutes (at 325°F). Use a cake tester to test for doneness. When done, remove tins from oven and remove cupcakes to a table or wire rack to cool.

LAYER-CAKE VARIATION: For a 9-inch round layer cake, pour batter into two generously oiled or greased and floured (or grease bottom and sides of pans and place waxed paper on pan bottoms) 9-inch round cake pans, and prepare six muffin cups (for cupcakes) with paper liners. Bake cupcakes at 325°F for 19 to 20 minutes or until a cake tester inserted in center comes out clean. Remove tin from oven and remove cupcakes to a wire rack to cool. Bake cake for 10 minutes longer or until a cake tester inserted in center of cake comes out clean. Remove pan from oven and place on a wire rack. Cool 10 minutes before loosening cake from sides of pan with a knife and removing cake from pan. Cool. Apply frosting of your choice between layers and on top. *Yield:* One 9-inch round layer cake plus 6 cupcakes

Quick Apple Upside-Down Cake

TOPPING

3 cups peeled, cored, and diced
  McIntosh apples

1 tablespoon vegetable oil
Scant 1 teaspoon cinnamon

CAKE

2 egg whites *or* 1 extralarge egg
¼ cup vegetable oil
½ teaspoon cinnamon
1 tablespoon unsweetened orange juice
  concentrate (Minute Maid Reduced
  Acid)

3 tablespoons unsweetened pineapple
  juice concentrate (Minute Maid)
½ cup unsweetened apple juice
  concentrate (any brand)
1½ cups all-purpose flour
1¼ teaspoons baking soda

1. Preheat oven to 350°F. Oil an 8- by 8- by 2-inch glass baking dish.

2. *To prepare topping:* In a large bowl, toss together apples, oil, and cinnamon. Spread mixture evenly into prepared baking dish.

3. In a large bowl, combine egg, oil, cinnamon, and concentrates; beat well by hand. Add flour and beat for 2 minutes by hand. Stir in baking soda quickly, and then mix (28 to 30 beats); immediately pour over apple mixture.

4. Bake 30 minutes at 350°F. Turn down oven to 325°F and bake 5 more minutes or until a cake tester inserted in center of cake comes out clean.

5. Remove baking dish from oven and place on a wire rack. Cool 20 minutes before loosening cake with a knife. Invert cake onto serving platter. Serve warm or cold. To store, place cooled cake in an airtight container and refrigerate or freeze.

Yield: One 8- by 8- by 2-inch cake (9 servings)

PER SERVING

Calories: 209
Protein: 3.1 g
Fat: 8.9 g
Carbohydrate: 31.6 g
Sodium: 135.4 mg

Diabetic exchanges
  Bread: 1
  Fat: 1½
  Fruit: 1

Apple Upside-Down Cake

No Egg

TOPPING

3 cups peeled, cored, and diced
   McIntosh apples

1 tablespoon vegetable oil
1 teaspoon cinnamon

BATTER

¼ cup vegetable oil
¼ teaspoon cinnamon
¼ cup unsweetened apple juice
   concentrate (any brand)
½ cup plus 2 tablespoons water
1½ teaspoons pure potato-starch flour
1½ cups plus 1 tablespoon all-purpose
   flour

2 tablespoons water
1½ teaspoons egg replacer (Ener-G
   brand)
1 teaspoon baking soda
2½ teaspoons baking powder

1. Preheat oven to 350°F. Oil an 8- by 8- by 2-inch glass baking dish.

2. *To prepare topping:* In a large bowl, toss together apples, oil, and cinnamon. Spread mixture evenly into prepared baking dish.

3. In a large bowl, combine oil, cinnamon, concentrate, water, and potato-starch flour; beat well. Add all-purpose flour and beat for 2 minutes by hand.

4. In a small bowl, and using a hand-operated mechanical beater, beat together water and egg replacer until bubbles form (mixture should not be thick or stiff). Pour egg-replacer mixture into flour-and-concentrate mixture and stir for 20 seconds by hand. Stir in baking soda and baking powder quickly, and then mix (28 to 30 beats); immediately pour mixture evenly over apple mixture.

5. Bake 30 minutes at 350°F. Turn oven down to 325°F and bake another 5 minutes or until a cake tester inserted in center of cake comes out clean.

6. Remove baking dish from oven and place on a wire rack. Cool 25 minutes before loosening cake with a knife. Invert cake onto serving platter. Serve warm or cold. To store, place cooled cake in an airtight container and refrigerate or freeze.

Yield: One 8- by 8- by 2-inch cake (9 servings)

Calories: 186   *Diabetic exchanges*
Protein: 2.3 g   Bread: 1
Fat: 7.9 g   Fat: 1½
Carbohydrate: 26.7 g   Fruit: ¾
Sodium: 186.6 mg

Pineapple-Cherry Upside-Down Cake

TOPPING

One 20-ounce can Dole unsweetened pineapple slices plus juice from the can

3 to 4 more Dole pineapple slices from a second can

26 unsweetened, frozen, and thawed dark sweet cherries

½ cup unsweetened pineapple juice concentrate (Minute Maid)

1 teaspoon water

3 tablespoons arrowroot or cornstarch

CAKE

2¼ cups all-purpose flour

1 cup date sugar, tapped well

1 tablespoon soy powder, dry milk powder, or all-purpose flour

⅔ cup vegetable oil

1 tablespoon water

1¼ cups unsweetened pineapple juice concentrate (Minute Maid) *or* ¾ cup

unsweetened apple juice concentrate plus ½ cup unsweetened pineapple juice concentrate

Generous ¼ teaspoon cinnamon

3 to 5 dashes nutmeg

8 egg whites *or* 4 extralarge eggs, beaten until quite foamy

2 teaspoons baking soda

1. Preheat oven to 325°F. Oil sides and bottoms of two 8- by 8- by 2-inch glass or ceramic baking dishes. Add 1 tablespoon more oil to the bottom of *each* dish and tip dish so the oil covers bottom evenly.

2. *To prepare topping:* Drain pineapple slices (reserving juice) and pat dry. Place thawed cherries on a paper towel and pat dry. Arrange pineapple slices in the bottoms of the baking dishes and place cherries in the centers of the pineapple rings and in between them.

3. In a small saucepan, combine concentrate, the juice from the can of pineapple, the water, and arrowroot. Heat, stirring constantly, over medium heat until mixture thickens. Remove mixture from heat and let cool.

4. When mixture is cool, spread it over arranged pineapple rings and cherries. Set aside.

5. *To prepare cake:* In a large bowl, stir together flour, date sugar, soy powder (or dry milk or flour), oil, water, and concentrate. Add cinnamon, nutmeg, and eggs and beat well by hand for 2 to 3 minutes. Stir in baking soda quickly, and then mix (28 to 30 beats); immediately pour batter over topping, dividing batter equally between the two baking dishes.

6. Bake 30 minutes at 325°F. Reduce oven to 300°F and continue baking 10 to 12 minutes or until a cake tester inserted in center of cake comes out clean.

7. Remove baking dishes from oven and place on wire racks. Cool 1 minute before loosening cakes with a knife. Invert cakes onto serving plates. Serve warm or cold. To store, place cooled cakes in airtight containers and refrigerate or freeze.

Yield: Two 8- by 8- by 2-inch cakes (18 servings)

PER SERVING

Calories: 246	*Diabetic exchanges*
Protein: 3.9 g	*Bread:* 1½
Fat: 8.2 g	*Fat:* 1½
Carbohydrate: 39.2 g	*Fruit:* 1
Sodium: 127.1 mg	

CUPCAKE VARIATION: This cake is very moist and therefore makes excellent cupcakes—except that you won't be using the topping. Follow the same instructions as for the cake, beginning at step #5. Preheat the oven to 325°F, fill 24 muffin cups with paper liners, and reduce the total baking time to only 16 to 18 minutes. Use a cake tester to test for doneness. When done, remove tins from oven and remove cupcakes to a table or wire rack to cool.

LAYER-CAKE VARIATIONS: For this layer cake, you won't be using the topping. Follow the same instructions as for the cake, beginning at step #5. Preheat the oven to 325°F.

For an 8- by 8- by 2-inch layer cake, generously oil two 8- by 8- by 2-inch glass or ceramic baking dishes. Bake 28 to 30 minutes, or until a cake tester inserted in center of cake comes out clean. Remove baking dishes from oven and place on a wire rack. Cool 10 minutes before loosening cakes from sides of dishes with a knife and inverting cakes from dishes. Cool. Apply frosting of your choice between layers and on top.

For a 9-inch round layer cake, pour batter into two generously oiled or greased (or grease bottom and sides of pans and place waxed paper on pan bottoms) 9-inch round cake pans. Bake at 325°F for 31 to 33 minutes or until a cake tester inserted in center of cake comes out clean. Remove pans from oven and place on a wire rack. Cool 10 minutes before loosening cakes from sides of pans with a knife and inverting cakes from pans. Cool. Apply frosting of your choice between layers and on top.

FRUIT
PIES

Because of their natural sweetness, apples, pears, peaches, pineapples, rhubarb, cherries, and blueberries all make delicious pie fillings. Try to use fresh fruit whenever possible, though frozen fruit works just as well if you are careful to drain it.

Of course, the secret to an outstanding pie is its crust. This chapter contains six different recipes for crusts, and I hope that from among them you will find at least one that works for you. Here are some hints that you may find useful in turning out the "perfect" pie:

- Make sure you drain the fruit well so that the filling does not become soggy.
- You may use a bit more or less of each fruit concentrate, depending on your taste. Three ounces of concentrate will result in a not-so-sweet pie; five or six ounces will result in a sweet pie. Just remember that if you use more concentrate than called for in a recipe, you may need to add more tapioca as a thickener.
- Pie crusts will be lighter and tenderer if you keep the dough cold until just before it goes in the oven. For this reason, I usually prepare the fruit filling first, then the topping (if I'm using a crumb-crust topping instead of a top crust), and finally the crust.
- Always grease your pie plates so that the crust does not stick to the bottom.
- Always cool pies thoroughly before storing them uncovered in the refrigerator, or cover and place them in the freezer.

60

No-Bake Graham-Cracker Crust

2 cups crushed Graham Cracker Cookie
   Cutouts (page 133)
3 tablespoons vegetable oil

1. In a medium-sized bowl, stir together graham-cracker crumbs and oil with a fork.

2. Pour mixture into an ungreased 9-inch pie plate and pat down by hand to form crust.

3. Fill crust with fruit pudding of choice (see pages 109–114). Do not bake.

Yield: One 9-inch pie crust (8 servings)

PER SERVING

Calories: 245   *Sodium:* 159.4 mg
Protein: 3.4 g   *Diabetic exchanges*
Fat: 14.8 g   *Bread:* 1½
Carbohydrate: 24.8 g   *Fat:* 3

Crust for a Double-Crust Pie

⅔ cup vegetable shortening of choice or cold lard with no preservatives or additives

2 cups all-purpose flour

1 teaspoon salt

4 to 7 tablespoons ice water

1. In a medium-sized bowl, combine shortening, flour, and salt. Using a fork or pastry cutter, cut up mixture until it resembles small peas.

2. Add ice water a little at a time, stirring gently with a fork until a soft dough ball is formed (see *Note*).

3. Cover dough and refrigerate until ready to use. (Be sure to use dough within 45 minutes to 1 hour.)

Yield: Enough dough for one 9-inch, double-crust pie (8 servings)

PER SERVING

Calories: 260
Protein: 3.3 g
Fat: 16.8 g
Carbohydrate: 23.8 g

Sodium: 244.9 mg
Diabetic exchanges
 Bread: 1½
 Fat: 3

Note: Recipe can be doubled, tripled, or quadrupled if making more than one pie. If you increase the recipe, do not make one large dough ball in step #2. Instead, make one dough ball for each crust by mixing the ice water with about 2 cups of the shortening/flour/salt mixture at a time. This allows you to handle the dough as little as possible, which helps keep the crust flaky and light.

Oil-Based Crust for a 9-Inch, Single-Crust Pie

1 cup all-purpose flour
Scant 3 tablespoons raw wheat germ
½ teaspoon salt

¼ cup plus 1 tablespoon plus ½
   teaspoon vegetable oil
2 tablespoons cold water

1. In a medium-sized bowl, stir together flour, wheat germ, and salt.

2. In a small bowl, stir together oil and water.

3. Pour liquid mixture over dry mixture and stir with a fork to form a soft dough.

4. Place dough on a sheet of waxed paper and flatten slightly with your hand. Cover dough with a second sheet of waxed paper and roll out dough to desired thickness of crust. Peel off top paper, turn dough over into an oiled 9-inch pie plate, and peel off second sheet of paper. Gently press dough into pie plate, fixing any rips and holes.

5. Add pie filling of choice. Add topping of choice (see pages 91–103) and bake according to directions for pie filling.

Yield: Enough dough for one 9-inch, single-crust pie (8 servings)

PER SERVING

Calories: 145
Protein: 2.4 g
Fat: 9.2 g
Carbohydrate: 13.2 g

Sodium: 122.5 mg
Diabetic exchanges
   Bread: ¾
   Fat: 2

Oil-Based Crust for a 9-Inch, Double-Crust Pie

2 cups all-purpose flour
Scant 6 tablespoons raw wheat germ
1 teaspoon salt

Scant ⅔ cup vegetable oil
4 tablespoons cold water

1. In a medium-sized bowl, stir together flour, wheat germ, and salt.

2. In a small bowl, stir together oil and water.

3. Pour liquid mixture over dry mixture and stir with a fork to form a soft dough. Divide dough in half.

4. Place one ball of dough on a sheet of waxed paper and flatten slightly with your hand. Cover dough with a second sheet of waxed paper and roll out to desired thickness of crust. Peel off top paper, turn dough over into an oiled 9-inch pie plate, and peel off second sheet of paper. Gently press dough into pie plate, fixing any rips and holes.

5. Add pie filling of choice. Flatten and roll out second half of dough as above. Place dough over pie filling, mending any rips and holes as best you can. Pinch layers together around edges and flute. Bake according to directions for pie filling.

Yield: Enough dough for one 9-inch, double-crust pie (8 servings)

PER SERVING

Calories: 274
Protein: 4.8 g
Fat: 16.5 g
Carbohydrate: 26.4 g

Sodium: 245.1 mg
Diabetic exchanges
  Bread: 1¼
  Fat: 3

Barley-Rice Pie Crust

1 cup barley flour
½ cup white-rice flour
½ teaspoon salt

3 tablespoons plus 1½ teaspoons
   vegetable shortening or lard
¼ cup plus 1 teaspoon water

1. Preheat oven to 350°F. Oil a 9-inch pie plate.

2. In a medium-sized bowl, stir together barley flour, rice flour, and salt. Add shortening and cut into flour mixture using a pastry cutter or a fork. Add water and mix well; mixture will be dry.

3. Pat dough into an oiled 9-inch pie plate. Make sure dough covers sides and bottom evenly. Press pastry to make edge. Add pie filling of choice (see pages 69–78). Place a crumb-crust topping (Barley-Rice Topping, page 92, is very good) over fruit and bake according to directions for pie filling.

Yield: One 9-inch pie crust (8 servings)

PER SERVING

Calories: 120
Protein: 2 g
Fat: 5.5 g
Carbohydrate: 16.4 g

Sodium: 170.2 g
Diabetic exchanges
  Bread: 1
  Fat: 1

Oatmeal Crust

1¼ cups oat flour
Generous ¼ teaspoon salt
2 tablespoons vegetable oil
4 to 4½ tablespoons water

1. Preheat oven to 350°F. Oil a 9-inch pie plate.

2. In a medium-sized bowl, stir together all ingredients with a fork.

3. Pat dough into prepared pie plate. Press pastry between fingers to make an edge. Add pie filling of choice (see pages 69–78); place a crumb-crust topping (see pages 91–103) over fruit and bake according to directions for pie filling.

4. If baking pie crust alone, use fork to prick bottom in several places to prevent buckling. Bake 18 to 20 minutes or until crust is golden.

Yield: One 9-inch pie crust (8 servings)

PER SERVING

Calories: 93
Protein: 2.7 g
Fat: 4.3 g
Carbohydrate: 11.6 g

Sodium: 61.5 mg
Diabetic exchanges
　Bread: ¾
　Fat: ¾

Prebaked Rice Pie Crust

1 cup white-rice flour or brown-rice flour

½ teaspoon salt

¼ cup vegetable oil

¼ cup plus 1 tablespoon plus ½ teaspoon cold water

1. Preheat oven to 350°F. Oil a 9-inch pie plate.

2. In a medium-sized bowl, stir together flour and salt. Add oil and water and gently mix with a fork to form dough. Dough will be dry and crumbly. Transfer to prepared pie plate and gently pat out dough to cover bottom and sides.

3. Bake about 16 minutes or until crust is off-white in color. Do not overbake or the crust will crack.

4. Remove pie plate from oven and place on a wire rack to cool for at least 20 minutes.

5. Cook pie filling of choice on top of stove. When filling is done, pour it into prebaked shell. Serve warm or cold.

Yield: Enough dough for one 9-inch, single-crust pie (8 servings)

PER SERVING

Calories: 115
Protein: 1.0 g
Fat: 6.8 g
Carbohydrate: 12.5 g

Sodium: 123.4 g
Diabetic exchanges
  Bread: ¼
  Fat: 1⅓

Mixed Granola Pie Crust

1¼ cups rolled oats
½ cup all-purpose flour or oat flour
⅔ cup unsweetened coconut,
    premoistened with 2 teaspoons water
    and 2 teaspoons vegetable oil
⅔ cup chopped nuts

Scant ¼ cup sesame seeds
2 teaspoons poppy seeds
½ teaspoon cinnamon
3 tablespoons sunflower seeds
7 tablespoons vegetable oil

1. Oil a 10-inch pie plate.

2. In a large bowl, stir together all ingredients with a fork. Set aside 1 cup (packed) of mixture for topping.

3. Press remaining mixture into bottom of prepared pie plate. Spread mixture over bottom and sides of plate, pressing firmly. Add pie filling of choice. Sprinkle 1 cup of reserved mixture over top of pie filling. Bake according to directions for pie filling.

Yield: One 10-inch pie crust plus topping (8 servings)

PER SERVING (USING PECANS FOR CHOPPED NUTS)

Calories: 315
Protein: 5.2 g
Fat: 26.9 g
Carbohydrate: 16.9 g

Sodium: 3.1 mg
Diabetic exchanges
  Bread: 1
  Fat: 5

Apple or Pear Pie

4 cups peeled, cored, and sliced apples
  or pears
½ teaspoon cinnamon
2 to 2½ tablespoons tapioca
2 tablespoons vegetable shortening,
  vegetable oil, or lard
½ to ¾ cup unsweetened pineapple
  juice concentrate (Minute Maid) or
  unsweetened apple juice concentrate
  (any brand)

One 9-inch pie shell of choice (see
  pages 61–68) plus top crust or
  topping of choice (see pages 91–103)

1. Preheat oven to 350°F.

2. In a large bowl, stir together fruit, cinnamon, tapioca, shortening, and concentrate; allow mixture to sit for 10 minutes. Pour mixture into pie shell of choice and add topping or crust of choice.

3. Bake 1 hour or until topping or crust is golden.

4. Remove pie from oven and place on a wire rack to cool. Serve warm or cold. To store, place cooled pie uncovered in refrigerator or place in an airtight container and freeze.

Yield: One 9-inch pie (8 servings)

PER SERVING (FILLING ONLY)

Calories: 99
Protein: 0.4 g
Fat: 3.2 g
Carbohydrate: 18.3 g

Sodium: 6.7 mg
Diabetic exchanges
  Fat: ½
  Fruit: 1¼

Blueberry Pie

Two 16-ounce packages frozen
   blueberries, thawed and drained
⅓ cup peeled, pitted, and sliced peaches
   (*do not pack*)
2 tablespoons vegetable oil
2 tablespoons water

2 tablespoons tapioca
¼ teaspoon lemon juice
One 9-inch pie shell of choice (see
   pages 61–68) plus top crust or
   topping of choice (see pages 91–103)

1. Preheat oven to 450°F.

2. Puree ½ cup blueberries, the peaches, oil, and water in blender. In a large bowl, stir together fruit puree, remaining blueberries, tapioca, and lemon juice; allow mixture to sit for 10 to 15 minutes. Pour mixture into pie shell of choice and add topping or crust of choice.

3. Bake at 450°F for 15 minutes. Reduce oven to 350°F and continue baking for 35 minutes or until topping or crust is golden.

4. Remove pie plate from oven and place on a wire rack to cool. Serve warm or cold. To store, place cooled pie uncovered in refrigerator or place in an airtight container and freeze.

Yield: One 9-inch pie (8 servings)

PER SERVING (FILLING ONLY)

Calories: 111
Protein: 0.8 g
Fat: 4.3 g
Carbohydrate: 19.8 g

Sodium: 7.1 mg
Diabetic exchanges
   Fat: ¾
   Fruit: 1⅓

Blueberry-Prune Pie

⅓ cup sliced peaches (*do not pack*)
10 pitted prunes (medium)
2 tablespoons water
1½ tablespoons vegetable oil
Two 16-ounce packages blueberries,
   thawed and drained

2 tablespoons tapioca
One 9-inch pie shell of choice (see
   pages 61–68) plus top crust or
   topping of choice (see pages 91–103)

1. Preheat oven to 450°F.

2. Puree peaches, prunes, water, and oil in a blender.

3. In a large bowl, stir together fruit puree, blueberries, and tapioca; allow mixture to sit for 10 minutes. Pour mixture into pie shell of choice and add topping or crust of choice.

4. Bake at 450°F for 15 minutes. Reduce oven to 350°F and continue baking for 35 minutes or until topping or crust is golden.

5. Remove pie plate from oven and place on a wire rack to cool. Serve warm or cold. To store, place cooled pie uncovered in refrigerator or place in an airtight container and freeze.

Yield: One 9-inch pie (8 servings)

PER SERVING (FILLING ONLY)

Calories: 131	*Sodium:* 7.6 mg
Protein: 1.1 g	*Diabetic exchanges*
Fat: 3.4 g	*Fat:* ¾
Carbohydrate: 27.1 g	*Fruit:* 1¼

Cherry-Peach Pie

Two 16-ounce packages frozen dark
    sweet cherries, thawed and drained
½ cup peeled, pitted, and sliced
    peaches, patted dry (*do not pack*)
2 tablespoons unsweetened pineapple
    juice concentrate (Minute Maid)

2 tablespoons vegetable oil
¼ teaspoon lemon juice
1½ to 2 tablespoons tapioca
One 9-inch pie shell of choice (see
    pages 61–68) plus top crust or
    topping of choice (see pages 91–103)

1. Preheat oven to 450°F.

2. Puree 12 of the cherries, the peaches, concentrate, and oil in a blender. In a large bowl, stir together fruit puree, remaining cherries, lemon juice, and tapioca; allow mixture to sit for 10 minutes. Pour mixture into pie shell of choice and add topping or crust of choice.

3. Bake at 450°F for 15 minutes. Reduce oven to 350°F and continue baking for 35 minutes or until topping or crust is golden.

4. Remove pie plate from oven and place on a wire rack to cool. Serve warm or cold. To store, place cooled pie uncovered in refrigerator or place in an airtight container and freeze.

Yield: One 9-inch pie (8 servings)

PER SERVING (FILLING ONLY)

Calories: 130
Protein: 1.5 g
Fat: 4.6 g
Carbohydrate: 23.4 g

Sodium: 2.2 mg
Diabetic exchanges
  Fat: 1
  Fruit: 1½

Cherry-Prune Pie

Two 16-ounce packages frozen dark
   sweet cherries, thawed and drained
8 pitted prunes (medium)
2 tablespoons vegetable oil
2 tablespoons unsweetened pineapple
   juice concentrate (Minute Maid) or
   apple juice concentrate (any brand)

1 tablespoon water
¼ teaspoon lemon juice
1½ to 2 tablespoons tapioca
One 9-inch pie shell of choice (see
   pages 61–68) plus top crust or
   topping of choice (see pages 91–103)

1. Preheat oven to 450°F.

2. Puree 12 of the cherries, the prunes, oil, concentrate, and water in a blender.

3. In a large bowl, stir together fruit puree, remaining cherries, lemon juice, and tapioca; allow mixture to sit for 10 minutes. Pour mixture into pie shell of choice and add topping or crust of choice.

4. Bake at 450°F for 15 minutes. Reduce oven to 350°F and continue baking for 35 minutes or until topping or crust is golden.

5. Remove pie plate from oven and place on a wire rack to cool. Serve warm or cold. To store, place cooled pie uncovered in refrigerator or place in an airtight container and freeze.

Yield: One 9-inch pie (8 servings)

PER SERVING (FILLING ONLY)

Calories: 146
Protein: 1.6 g
Fat: 4.6 g
Carbohydrate: 27.5 g

Sodium: 2.4 mg
Diabetic exchanges
  Fat: 1
  Fruit: 1¾

Mixed Granola Pie

2 cups peeled, pitted, and sliced peaches
1 pear, peeled, cored, and diced
1 cup frozen blueberries, thawed and
   drained
½ cup frozen red raspberries, thawed
   and drained
½ cup frozen black raspberries, thawed
   and drained
2 plums, peeled, pitted, and diced

4 tablespoons tapioca
1 tablespoon vegetable oil
½ teaspoon lemon juice
½ teaspoon cinnamon
One 10-inch Mixed Granola Pie Crust
   (page 68) or pie shell of choice (see
   pages 61–68) plus top crust or
   topping of choice (see pages 91–103)

1. Preheat oven to 350°F.

2. In a large bowl, stir together all ingredients and allow mixture to sit for 10 minutes.

3. Pour mixture into Mixed Granola Pie Crust. Sprinkle granola topping over filling or use crust or topping of choice.

4. Bake 1 hour or until crust or topping is golden.

5. Remove pie from oven and place on a wire rack to cool. Serve warm or cold. To store, place cooled pie uncovered in refrigerator or place in an airtight container and freeze.

Yield: One 10-inch pie (8 servings)

PER SERVING (FILLING ONLY)

Calories: 85
Protein: 0.7 g
Fat: 2.1 g
Carbohydrate: 17.4 g

Sodium: 1.6 mg
Diabetic exchanges
   Fat: ½
   Fruit: 1

Peach Pie

4 cups peeled, pitted, and sliced peaches
½ teaspoon cinnamon
4 to 4½ tablespoons tapioca
2 tablespoons vegetable shortening,
  vegetable oil, or lard
½ to ¾ cup unsweetened pineapple
  juice concentrate (Minute Maid) or
  unsweetened apple juice concentrate
  (any brand)

One 9-inch pie shell of choice (see
  pages 61–68) plus top crust or
  topping of choice (see pages 91–103)

1. Preheat oven to 350°F.

2. In a large bowl, stir together peaches, cinnamon, tapioca, shortening, and concentrate; allow mixture to sit for 10 minutes. Pour mixture into pie shell of choice and add topping or crust of choice.

3. Bake 1 hour or until topping or crust is golden.

4. Remove pie from oven and place on a wire rack to cool. Serve warm or cold. To store, place cooled pie uncovered in refrigerator or place in an airtight container and freeze.

Yield: One 9-inch pie (8 servings)

PER SERVING (FILLING ONLY)

Calories: 112	*Sodium:* 6.9 mg
Protein: 0.9 g	*Diabetic exchanges*
Fat: 3.1 g	*Fat:* ¼
Carbohydrate: 21.5 g	*Fruit:* 1⅓

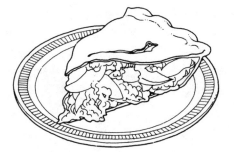

Raspberry-Peach Pie

¾ to 1 cup fresh or frozen, thawed, and drained red raspberries

2 tablespoons water

3 to 4 peaches, peeled, pitted, and sliced

¼ to ⅓ cup unsweetened pineapple juice concentrate (Minute Maid)

3 tablespoons tapioca

1 tablespoon vegetable shortening, vegetable oil, or lard

2 tablespoons *dry* coconut (optional)

One 9-inch pie shell of choice (see pages 61–68) plus top crust or topping of choice (see pages 91–103)

1. Preheat oven to 350°F.

2. Puree raspberries and water in a blender. Strain puree through a small hand strainer, discarding seeds.

3. In a large bowl, stir together puree, peaches, concentrate, tapioca, shortening, and coconut; allow mixture to sit for 5 minutes. Pour mixture into pie shell of choice and add topping or crust of choice.

4. Bake 1 hour or until topping or crust is golden.

5. Remove pie from oven and place on a wire rack to cool. Serve warm or cold. To store, place cooled pie uncovered in refrigerator or place in an airtight container and freeze.

Yield: One 9-inch pie (8 servings)

PER SERVING (FILLING ONLY)

Calories: 61
Protein: 0.5 g
Fat: 1.6 g
Carbohydrate: 11.9 g

Sodium: 3.2 mg
Diabetic exchanges
 Fat: ¼
 Fruit: ¾

Rhubarb-Pineapple Pie

1 cup plus 2 tablespoons (9 ounces)
  unsweetened pineapple juice
  concentrate (Minute Maid)
6 tablespoons tapioca
2 tablespoons vegetable shortening,
  vegetable oil, or lard

1 quart chopped rhubarb
One 9-inch pie shell of choice (see
  pages 61–68) plus top crust or
  topping (see pages 91–103)

1. Preheat oven to 350°F.

2. In a large bowl, stir together concentrate, tapioca, shortening, and rhubarb; allow mixture to sit for 10 minutes.

3. Pour mixture into pie shell of choice. Top with crust or topping of choice.

4. Bake 60 to 70 minutes or until crust or topping is golden.

5. Remove pie plate from oven and place on a wire rack to cool. Serve warm or cold. To store, place cooled pie uncovered in refrigerator, or place in an airtight container and freeze.

Yield: One 9-inch pie (8 servings)

PER SERVING (FILLING ONLY)

Calories: 138
Protein: 1.2 g
Fat: 3.1 g
Carbohydrate: 26.8 g
Sodium: 16.6 mg

Diabetic exchanges
  Bread: ½
  Fat: ¾
  Fruit: 1

Pumpkin Pie

No Egg
No Dairy

Prebaked Rice Pie Crust (see *Note;* see
page 67) or 9-inch pie shell of choice
(see pages 61–68)
5 tablespoons white-rice flour
4 tablespoons water
1 tablespoon vegetable oil
One 16-ounce can solid-pack pumpkin
(Libby's 100% Natural)

¾ cup brown-rice syrup
½ teaspoon salt
1 teaspoon cinnamon
½ teaspoon ginger
¼ teaspoon cloves
½ cup water
1½ teaspoons baking powder

1. Preheat oven to 375°F.

2. In a large bowl, stir together rice flour, water, and oil. Add pumpkin, rice syrup, salt, cinnamon, ginger, cloves, and water; mix well. Stir in baking powder quickly, and then mix (28 to 30 beats); immediately pour filling into pie shell.

3. Bake 25 minutes; turn down oven to 350°F and bake pie another 45 minutes or until crust is golden and top of pie becomes a little dark and looks as if it has a "skin" on it. A knife inserted in the center of the pie will *not come out clean* and *will not be an accurate test for doneness.* Also, this pie will thicken as it cools.

4. Remove pie from oven and place on a wire rack to cool. Serve warm or cold. To store, place cooled pie uncovered in refrigerator or place in an airtight container and freeze.

Yield: One 9-inch pie (8 servings)

PER SERVING (FILLING ONLY)

Calories: 117
Protein: 1.1 g
Fat: 2.0 g
Carbohydrate: 24.3 g
Sodium: 189.3 mg

Diabetic exchanges
Bread: ½
Fat: ½
Fruit: 1

Note: With this pie filling, prebake Rice Pie Crust for only 10 minutes, then pour filling into shell and bake for specified time stated for pie filling. This direction only concerns the Prebaked Rice Pie Crust.

FRUIT CRISPS AND TOPPINGS

Fruit crisps make wonderful desserts. They call for fresh natural produce (but you may substitute frozen fruit if fresh is not available), they are simple and quick to prepare (no crust necessary, as with pies), and they can be served warm right from the baking dish. Here are just a few hints for making your crisps "crispy" and delicious:

- Make sure you drain the fruit well.
- You may use a bit more or less of each fruit concentrate, depending on desired sweetness. Just remember that if you use more concentrate than called for in a recipe, you may need to add more tapioca as the thickener.
- When a recipe calls for *dry* coconut, do not premoisten it; the coconut will get its moisture from the fruit.
- Too much shortening or lard in a topping will make it too wet; not enough will make it too dry. As this is very much a matter of taste, you may need to experiment with the lard/shortening quantities in the toppings until you get the desired result.
- A topping made of just flour, shortening, and cinnamon does not work well. You need to add coconut or seeds or chopped nuts or rolled oats (or all these things) to make a good topping. Feel free to experiment with the recipes in this chapter and create your own unique topping.
- When lard or shortening is used in the fruit filling, be sure to melt it before mixing it with the fruit; otherwise, you may get a wet spot under the topping.
- Whenever possible, bake your crisps in glass or ceramic baking dishes rather than in metal baking pans. A glass dish makes a more attractive serving dish, and, even if you refrigerate the crisp for a day or two, a glass dish won't become stained; nor will there be a chemical reaction with the acid from the fruit.

80

Fruit-Berry Crisp

2 cups peeled, pitted, and diced peaches
¾ cup fresh or frozen, thawed, and
    drained red raspberries
¾ cup fresh or frozen, thawed, and
    drained blueberries

Scant ½ teaspoon cinnamon
4 tablespoons tapioca
Crispy Oat Topping (see page 94) or
    topping of choice

1. Preheat oven to 350°F. Oil a 9- by 9- by 2-inch glass or ceramic baking dish.

2. In a large bowl, stir together all ingredients. Spread fruit in prepared dish. Let sit 10 minutes. Add topping.

3. Bake 1 hour or until topping is crisp looking and slightly golden.

4. Remove dish from oven and place on a wire rack to cool. Serve warm or cold. Store uncovered cooled crisp in refrigerator. Freeze in portions.

Yield: 9 servings

PER SERVING (WITHOUT TOPPING)

Calories: 42
Protein: 0.4 g
Fat: 0.2 g
Carbohydrate: 10.4 g

Sodium: 1.0 mg
Diabetic exchanges
    Fruit: ⅔

Mixed Fruit Crisp

1 large or 2 small pears, peeled, cored, and sliced

2 peaches, peeled, pitted, and sliced (1 cup)

1 large or 2 small nectarines, peeled and sliced (1 cup)

2 large or 3 small plums, diced

10 dark, sweet, seedless cherries

Generous ½ cup fresh or frozen, thawed, and drained red raspberries

Generous ½ cup fresh or frozen, thawed, and drained black raspberries

Generous ½ cup fresh or frozen, thawed, and drained blueberries

⅓ cup chopped rhubarb

5 tablespoons tapioca

¼ teaspoon cinnamon

1 tablespoon vegetable shortening (melted), vegetable oil, or lard (melted)

Sesame Topping (see page 99) or topping of choice

1. Preheat oven to 350°F. Oil a 13- by 9- by 2-inch glass or ceramic baking dish.

2. In a large bowl, stir together all fruit and rhubarb. Add tapioca, cinnamon, and shortening; stir well. Spread fruit in prepared dish and add topping.

3. Bake 1 hour or until topping is crisp looking and slightly golden.

4. Remove dish from oven and place on a wire rack to cool. Serve warm or cold. Store uncovered cooled crisp in refrigerator. Freeze in portions.

Yield: 15 servings

PER SERVING (WITHOUT TOPPING)

Calories: 53
Protein: 0.6 g
Fat: 1.1 g
Carbohydrate: 11.5 g

Sodium: 0.3 mg
Diabetic exchanges
  Fat: ¼
  Fruit: ¾

Apple or Pear Crisp

4 cups peeled, cored, and diced apple or pear

½ teaspoon cinnamon

2½ tablespoons tapioca

2 tablespoons vegetable oil

½ cup unsweetened pineapple juice concentrate (Minute Maid) or unsweetened apple juice concentrate (any brand)

Pecan Topping (see page 96), Whole-Wheat 'n' Walnut Topping (see page 102), or topping of choice

1. Preheat oven to 350°F. Oil a 9- by 9- by 2-inch glass or ceramic baking dish.

2. In a large bowl, stir together all ingredients except topping. Pour mixture in prepared dish and add topping.

3. Bake 1 hour or until topping is crisp looking and slightly golden.

4. Remove dish from oven and place on a wire rack to cool. Serve warm or cold. Store uncovered cooled crisp in refrigerator. Freeze in portions.

Yield: 9 servings

PER SERVING (WITHOUT TOPPING)

Calories: 93
Protein: 0.3 g
Fat: 3.2 g
Carbohydrate: 16.7 g

Sodium: 6.0 mg
Diabetic exchanges
 Fat: ½
 Fruit: 1¼

Blueberry Crisp

¾ cup fresh blueberries
3 tablespoons water
2 cups fresh or frozen, thawed, and
  drained blueberries

3 tablespoons tapioca
1 tablespoon vegetable oil
Barley Topping (see page 91) or topping
  of choice

1. Preheat oven to 350°F. Oil a 9- by 9- by 2-inch glass or ceramic baking dish.
2. Puree ¾ cup blueberries and water in a blender.
3. In a large bowl, stir together blueberry puree and remaining blueberries. Stir in tapioca and oil. Pour mixture into prepared baking dish and let sit for 10 minutes. Add topping.
4. Bake 50 minutes or until topping is crisp looking and slightly golden.
5. Remove dish from oven and place on a wire rack to cool. Serve warm or cold. Store uncovered cooled crisp in refrigerator. Freeze in portions.

Yield: 9 servings

PER SERVING (WITHOUT TOPPING)

Calories: 51
Protein: 0.3 g
Fat: 1.9 g
Carbohydrate: 9.3 g

Sodium: 2.7 mg
Diabetic exchanges
  Fat: ⅓
  Fruit: ⅔

Cherry Crisp

2 cups fresh or frozen, thawed, and
   drained dark sweet cherries
2 tablespoons vegetable oil
3 tablespoons plus 1½ teaspoons
   tapioca

⅓ to ½ cup unsweetened pineapple
   juice concentrate (Minute Maid)
2 tablespoons water
Double-Oat Topping (see page 95) or
   topping of choice

1. Preheat oven to 350°F. Oil a 9- by 9- by 2-inch glass or ceramic baking dish.

2. In a large bowl, stir together all ingredients except topping. Pour mixture into prepared baking dish and let sit for 10 minutes. Add topping.

3. Bake 50 minutes or until topping is crisp looking and slightly golden.

4. Remove dish from oven and place on a wire rack to cool. Serve warm or cold. Store uncovered cooled crisp in refrigerator. Freeze in portions.

Yield: 9 servings

PER SERVING (WITHOUT TOPPING)

Calories: 79
Protein: 0.5 g
Fat: 3.3 g
Carbohydrate: 12.4 g

Sodium: 3.9 mg
Diabetic exchanges
   Fat: ¼
   Fruit: ¾

Peach Crisp

4 cups peeled, pitted, and thinly sliced
  peaches
5 tablespoons tapioca
2 tablespoons vegetable shortening
  (melted), vegetable oil, or lard
  (melted)
½ cup unsweetened pineapple juice
  concentrate (Minute Maid) or
  unsweetened apple juice concentrate
  (any brand)

½ teaspoon cinnamon
Pecan Topping (see page 96) or topping
  of choice

1. Preheat oven to 350°F. Oil a 9- by 9- by 2-inch glass or ceramic baking dish.

2. Drain peaches well and pat dry with a paper towel.

3. In a large bowl, stir together all ingredients except topping. Pour into prepared baking dish and let sit for 10 minutes. Add topping.

4. Bake 1 hour or until topping is crisp looking and slightly golden.

5. Remove dish from oven and place on a wire rack to cool. Serve warm or cold. Store uncovered cooled crisp in refrigerator. Freeze in portions.

Yield: 9 servings

PER SERVING (WITHOUT TOPPING)

Calories: 101
Protein: 0.7 g
Fat: 2.9 g
Carbohydrate: 18.7 g

Sodium: 6.1 mg
Diabetic exchanges
  Fat: ½
  Fruit: 1¼

Peaches 'n' Berries Crisp

⅓ cup fresh or frozen, thawed, and
   drained red raspberries
⅓ cup fresh or frozen, thawed, and
   drained black raspberries
4 tablespoons water
3½ cups peeled, pitted, and sliced
   peaches

1 tablespoon vegetable oil
½ teaspoon cinnamon
Generous 5 tablespoons tapioca
Wheat Germ Topping (see page 101) or
   topping of choice

1. Preheat oven to 350°F. Oil a 9- by 9- by 2-inch glass or ceramic baking dish.

2. Puree red and black raspberries and water in blender. Press puree through strainer and discard seeds.

3. In a large bowl, stir together raspberry puree, peaches, oil, cinnamon, and tapioca. Pour mixture into prepared dish and add topping.

4. Bake 50 to 55 minutes or until topping is crisp looking and slightly golden.

5. Remove dish from oven and place on a wire rack to cool. Serve warm or cold. Store uncovered cooled crisp in refrigerator. Freeze in portions.

Yield: 9 servings

PER SERVING (WITHOUT TOPPING)

Calories: 62
Protein: 0.5 g
Fat: 1.6 g
Carbohydrate: 11.9 g

Sodium: 0.4 mg
Diabetic exchanges
  Fat: ¼
  Fruit: ¾

Pear Crisp

4 cups peeled, cored, and diced pears
  (set aside ¼ cup)
1¼ cups peeled, pitted, and sliced
  peaches
½ teaspoon cinnamon
3 tablespoons plus 1½ teaspoons
  tapioca
2 tablespoons vegetable shortening
  (melted), vegetable oil, or lard
  (melted)

2 tablespoons *dry*, unsweetened coconut
  or 1 tablespoon poppy or sesame
  seeds *or* 2 tablespoons chopped nuts
Nutty Nutmeg Topping (see page 93),
  Barley-Cashew Topping (see page
  92), or topping of choice

1. Preheat oven to 350°F. Oil a 9- by 9- by 2-inch glass or ceramic baking dish.
2. Puree ¼ cup pears and the peaches in a blender.
3. In a large bowl, stir together remaining 3¾ cups diced pears, pureed fruit, cinnamon, tapioca, shortening, and coconut (or seeds or nuts). Pour mixture into prepared dish and let sit for 10 minutes. Add topping.
4. Bake 1 hour or until topping is crisp looking and slightly golden.
5. Remove dish from oven and place on a wire rack to cool. Serve warm or cold. Store uncovered cooled crisp in refrigerator. Freeze in portions.

Yield: 9 servings

PER SERVING (WITHOUT TOPPING)

Calories: 83
Protein: 0.5 g
Fat: 3.3 g
Carbohydrate: 14.2 g

Sodium: 0.8 mg
Diabetic exchanges
  Fat: ½
  Fruit: 1

Pineapple Crisp

One 20-ounce can unsweetened
  pineapple rings (use Dole if you are
  allergic to phenol)
2 cups peeled and diced nectarines
½ cup peeled, pitted, and diced plums,
  patted dry

⅓ cup unsweetened pineapple juice
  concentrate (Minute Maid)
4 tablespoons tapioca
½ teaspoon cinnamon
Potato Topping (see page 97) or topping
  of choice

1. Preheat oven to 350°F. Oil a 9- by 9- by 2-inch glass or ceramic baking dish.
2. Drain pineapple slices and pat dry. Chop into bite-sized pieces.
3. In a large bowl, stir together all ingredients except topping. Pour mixture into prepared baking dish and add topping.
4. Bake 50 to 55 minutes or until topping is crisp looking and slightly golden.
5. Remove baking dish from oven and place on a wire rack to cool. Serve warm or cold. Store uncovered cooled crisp in refrigerator. Freeze in portions.

Yield: 9 servings

PER SERVING (WITHOUT TOPPING)

Calories: 101
Protein: 0.8 g
Fat: 0.3 g
Carbohydrate: 25.1 g

Sodium: 9.3 mg
Diabetic exchanges
  Fruit: 1¼

Pineapple-Rhubarb Crisp

3 cups chopped rhubarb
1 tablespoon vegetable oil
⅓ cup plus 1 tablespoon tapioca
1½ cups unsweetened pineapple juice
  concentrate (Minute Maid)
One 20-ounce can unsweetened
  pineapple rings (use Dole if you are
  allergic to phenol), cut up and
  drained

¼ cup *dry* unsweetened coconut
  (optional)
Whole-Wheat and Sesame Topping (see
  page 103) or topping of choice

1. Preheat oven to 350°F. Oil a 10- by 8- by 2-inch glass or ceramic baking dish.

2. In a large bowl, stir together all ingredients except topping. Pour mixture into prepared baking dish and let sit for 10 minutes. Add topping.

3. Bake 60 to 65 minutes or until topping is crisp looking and slightly golden.

4. Remove dish from oven and place on a wire rack to cool. Serve warm or cold. Store uncovered cooled crisp in refrigerator. Freeze in portions.

Yield: 9 servings

PER SERVING (WITHOUT TOPPING)

Calories: 168
Protein: 1.1 g
Fat: 1.6 g
Carbohydrate: 37.9 g

Sodium: 24.0 g
Diabetic exchanges
  Fat: ¼
  Fruit: 2½

Barley Topping

¼ cup pearled barley
3 tablespoons barley flour
1 tablespoon sesame seeds
2 tablespoons vegetable oil
1 tablespoon water
Optional: ¼ cup unsweetened coconut,
    premoistened with 1 teaspoon water
    and 1 teaspoon vegetable oil; *or* ¼
    cup seeds; *or* ¼ cup chopped nuts; *or*
    ¼ cup rolled oats; *or* any
    combination of the above

1. In a medium-sized bowl, stir together all ingredients.
2. Spoon on top of any pie or fruit mixture.

Yield: Enough topping for one crisp or one 9-inch pie (8.5 servings)

PER SERVING

Calories: 103
Protein: 1.9 g
Fat: 3.9 g
Carbohydrate: 15.7 g

Sodium: 0.9 mg
Diabetic exchanges
  Bread: 1
  Fat: ¾

Barley-Cashew Topping

¾ cup pearled barley
¼ cup chopped cashews
3 tablespoons barley flour

¼ teaspoon cinnamon
2 tablespoons vegetable oil

1. In a medium-sized bowl, stir together all ingredients.
2. Spoon topping over any pie or fruit mixture and smooth topping by hand.

Yield: Enough topping for one crisp or one 9-inch pie (8.5 servings)

PER SERVING

Calories: 119
Protein: 2.3 g
Fat: 5.0 g
Carbohydrate: 16.8 g

Sodium: 0.5 mg
Diabetic exchanges
  Bread: 1
  Fat: 1

Barley-Rice Topping

¼ to ⅓ cup pearled barley
3 tablespoons white-rice flour
3 tablespoons barley flour
½ cup chopped nuts

¼ to ½ teaspoon cinnamon
Generous 1 tablespoon vegetable
  shortening or lard

1. In a medium-sized bowl, stir together all ingredients with a fork.
2. Spoon topping over any pie or fruit mixture and smooth topping by hand gently.

Yield: Enough topping for one 9-inch pie or one crisp (8.5 servings)

PER SERVING (IF USING PECANS FOR CHOPPED NUTS)

Calories: 91
Protein: 1.4 g
Fat: 6.3 g
Carbohydrate: 8.7 g

Sodium: 0.3 mg
Diabetic exchanges
  Bread: ½
  Fat: 1¼

Nutty Nutmeg Topping

¾ cup all-purpose flour
⅓ cup chopped nuts of choice
1½ tablespoons unsweetened coconut,
   premoistened with ½ teaspoon water
   and ½ teaspoon vegetable oil
   (optional)

1½ teaspoons sesame seeds
4 tablespoons vegetable shortening or
   lard
¼ teaspoon cinnamon
⅛ teaspoon nutmeg

1. In a medium-sized bowl, mix all ingredients with a fork.
2. Spoon topping over any pie or fruit mixture and smooth topping by hand.

Yield: Enough topping for one crisp or one 9-inch pie (8.5 servings)

PER SERVING (USING PECANS FOR CHOPPED NUTS)

Calories: 126
Protein: 1.6 g
Fat: 9.6 g
Carbohydrate: 9.8 g
Sodium: 0.4 mg

Diabetic exchanges
  Bread: ½
  Fat: 2

Crispy Oat Topping

⅓ cup all-purpose flour
½ cup rolled oats
Optional: ⅓ cup unsweetened coconut, premoistened with 1½ teaspoons water and 1½ teaspoons vegetable oil; *or* ⅓ cup raw, hulled sunflower seeds; *or* ⅓ cup chopped nuts

4 tablespoons vegetable shortening or lard
¼ teaspoon cinnamon

1. In a medium-sized bowl, mix all ingredients with a fork.
2. Spoon topping over any pie or fruit mixture and smooth topping by hand.

Yield: Enough topping for one crisp or one 9-inch pie (8.5 servings)

PER SERVING

Calories: 87
Protein: 1.4 g
Fat: 6.1 g
Carbohydrate: 7.3 g

Sodium: 0.1 mg
Diabetic exchanges
  Bread: ½
  Fat: 1

Double-Oat Topping

½ to ¾ cup rolled oats
¼ cup oat flour
3 tablespoons vegetable oil
2 tablespoons sesame seeds
⅛ to ¼ teaspoon cinnamon

Optional: ¼ cup unsweetened coconut, premoistened with 1 teaspoon water and 1 teaspoon vegetable oil; *or* ¼ cup seeds and ¼ cup chopped nuts

1. In a medium-sized bowl, stir together all ingredients with a fork.
2. Spoon topping over any pie or fruit mixture.

Yield: Enough topping for one crisp or one 9-inch pie (8.5 servings)

PER SERVING

Calories: 83
Protein: 1.9 g
Fat: 6.3 g
Carbohydrate: 5.5 g

Sodium: 0.8 mg
Diabetic exchanges
  Bread: ⅓
  Fat: 1¼

Pecan Topping

¾ cup all-purpose flour
⅓ cup chopped pecans
Generous ¼ teaspoon cinnamon
¼ cup vegetable shortening or lard

1. In a medium-sized bowl, stir together all ingredients.
2. Spoon topping over any pie or fruit mixture and smooth topping by hand.

Yield: Enough topping for one crisp or one 9-inch pie (8.5 servings)

PER SERVING

Calories: 123   *Sodium:* 0.3 mg
Protein: 1.5 g   *Diabetic exchanges*
Fat: 9.1 g   *Bread:* ½
Carbohydrate: 9.2 g   *Fat:* 2

Potato Topping

¼ cup plus 1 tablespoon potato flour
Generous ¼ teaspoon cinnamon
¼ cup chopped dried fruit of choice (cut up fruit with scissors)

¼ cup chopped walnuts or other nut of choice
1 tablespoon vegetable oil

1. In a medium-sized bowl, stir together potato flour, cinnamon, dried fruit, and nuts. Stir in oil.

2. Sprinkle topping over any pie or fruit.

Yield: Enough topping for one crisp or one 9-inch pie (8.5 servings)

PER SERVING

Calories: 69
Protein: 1.0 g
Fat: 3.7 g
Carbohydrate: 8.8 g
Sodium: 3.4 mg

Diabetic exchanges
  Bread: ⅓
  Fat: ½
  Fruit: ¼

Rice Topping

1 unsalted rice cake, crumbled
¼ cup plus 1 tablespoon white-rice
    flour
¼ cup roasted sunflower or roasted
    sesame seeds (optional)

Scant 2 tablespoons vegetable oil
⅛ to ¼ teaspoon allspice

1. In a medium-sized bowl, stir together all ingredients with a fork.
2. Spoon topping over any pie or fruit mixture and smooth topping by hand.

Yield: Enough topping for one crisp or one 9-inch pie (8.5 servings)

PER SERVING

Calories: 49
Protein: 0.4 g
Fat: 3.3 g
Carbohydrate: 4.5 g

Sodium: 0.4 mg
Diabetic exchanges
    Bread: ⅓
    Fat: ½

Sesame Topping

¾ to 1 cup all-purpose flour
1½ tablespoons sesame seeds
Optional: ⅓ cup unsweetened coconut,
   premoistened with 1½ teaspoons
   water and 1½ teaspoons vegetable oil
   plus 1 teaspoon poppy seeds; *or* ¼
   cup chopped nuts; *or* ¼ cup rolled
   oats; *or* any combination of above

¼ cup plus 1½ to 2 tablespoons
   vegetable shortening or lard
Generous ¼ teaspoon cinnamon

1. In a medium-sized bowl, mix all ingredients with a fork.
2. Spoon topping over any pie or fruit mixture and smooth topping by hand.

Yield: Enough for one 13- by 9- by 2-inch crisp (15 servings)

PER SERVING

Calories: 69
Protein: 0.8 g
Fat: 5.1 g
Carbohydrate: 4.9 g

Sodium: 0.4 mg
Diabetic exchanges
   Bread: ⅓
   Fat: 1

Roasted Sunflower Topping

⅓ cup roasted sunflower seeds
⅛ teaspoon cinnamon

1. In a small bowl, stir together sunflower seeds and cinnamon.
2. Sprinkle topping over any pie or fruit mixture.

Yield: Enough topping for one crisp or one 9-inch pie (8.5 servings)

PER SERVING

Calories: 34
Protein: 1.1 g
Fat: 2.9 g
Carbohydrate: 1.4 g

Sodium: 0
Diabetic exchange
  Fat: ¾

Super-Energy Topping

¾ cup rolled oats
⅓ cup oat flour
¼ cup chopped almonds or other nut of choice

2 tablespoons sesame seeds
1 teaspoon poppy seeds
3 tablespoons vegetable oil

1. In a medium-sized bowl, stir together all ingredients.
2. Spoon topping over any pie or fruit mixture and smooth topping by hand.

Yield: Enough topping for one crisp or one 9-inch pie (8.5 servings)

PER SERVING

Calories: 121
Protein: 3.3 g
Fat: 8.9 g
Carbohydrate: 8.8 g

Sodium: 1.4 mg
Diabetic exchanges
  Bread: ½
  Fat: 2

Wheat Germ Topping

½ cup all-purpose flour
3 tablespoons wheat germ
½ teaspoon cinnamon
2 tablespoons vegetable oil

Optional: ¼ cup unsweetened coconut, premoistened with 1 teaspoon water and 1 teaspoon vegetable oil; *or* ¼ cup seeds; *or* ¼ cup chopped nuts

1. In a medium-sized bowl, mix all ingredients with a fork.
2. Spoon topping over any pie or fruit mixture and smooth topping by hand.

Yield: Enough topping for one crisp or one 9-inch pie (8.5 servings)

PER SERVING

Calories: 68
Protein: 1.6 g
Fat: 3.5 g
Carbohydrate: 7.5 g

Sodium: 0.3 mg
Diabetic exchanges
   Bread: ½
   Fat: ¾

Whole-Wheat 'n' Walnut Topping

¾ cup whole-wheat flour
¼ cup chopped walnuts
¼ cup rolled oats

Generous ¼ teaspoon cinnamon
5 tablespoons vegetable shortening or
lard

1. In a medium-sized bowl, mix all ingredients with a fork.
2. Spoon topping over any pie or fruit mixture and smooth topping by hand.

Yield: Enough topping for one crisp or one 9-inch pie (8.5 servings)

PER SERVING

Calories: 131
Protein: 2.7 g
Fat: 10.1 g
Carbohydrate: 9.6 g

Sodium: 0.4 mg
Diabetic exchanges
  Bread: ½
  Fat: 2

Whole-Wheat and Sesame Topping

¾ cup whole-wheat flour
1 to 2 tablespoons sesame seeds
4 tablespoons vegetable shortening or
  lard
¼ to ½ teaspoon cinnamon

Optional: ⅓ cup unsweetened coconut,
  premoistened with 1½ teaspoons
  water and 1½ teaspoons vegetable
  oil; or ⅓ cup seeds; or ⅓ cup
  chopped nuts; or ⅓ cup rolled oats

1. In a medium-sized bowl, mix all ingredients with a fork.
2. Spoon topping over any pie or fruit mixture and smooth topping by hand.

Yield: Enough topping for one crisp or one 9-inch pie (8.5 servings)

PER SERVING

Calories: 93
Protein: 1.6 g
Fat: 6.9 g
Carbohydrate: 7.7 g

Sodium: 0.7 mg
Diabetic exchanges
  Bread: ½
  Fat: 1¼

FRUIT
SAUCES
AND
FRUIT
PUDDINGS

Puddings are versatile and delicious nonsugar treats. They can be served plain, with a sprinkling of unsweetened coconut or nuts or seeds; they can be used as a pie filling with No-Bake Graham-Cracker Crust (page 61); or they can be used as a topping for Apple-Cinnamon or Pear-Cinnamon Rolls (page 20).

The secret to making creamy, smooth pudding is to stir constantly once the thickener has been added. You must also make sure that you cook the pudding long enough for it to become thick. Pudding will usually splatter when it boils, so use a cover with vents, or only partially cover the saucepan.

THICKENERS

Arrowroot. This is my favorite thickener because it does not affect the taste of the pudding the way flour often does. When cooked over medium heat, arrowroot will thicken your fruit mixture *before* it reaches the boiling point, so make sure that you watch the mixture, stir constantly, and are careful not to overcook.

Cornstarch. Use this only if you are not allergic to corn. When cooked over medium heat, cornstarch will thicken your fruit mixture about one to two minutes after it reaches the boiling point. Be sure to stir constantly during the entire cooking time.

Flour. Flour may add its own flavor to your puddings. When cooked over medium heat, flour will thicken your fruit mixture about two to three minutes after it reaches the boiling point. Be sure to stir constantly during the entire cooking time.

Tapioca. Tapioca is similar to arrowroot in that it does not affect the taste of the fruit in your pudding. You should combine tapioca with fruit and concentrate in a small saucepan and allow to stand for five minutes. Stirring constantly, bring to a boil over medium heat. Boil one minute. Remove from heat and cool. Pudding thickens as it cools.

Equivalents

   2 tablespoons flour = 1 tablespoon arrowroot

   2 tablespoons flour = 1 tablespoon cornstarch

   1 tablespoon cornstarch = 2 tablespoons tapioca

Raspberry Tapioca Pudding

2 cups fresh or frozen, thawed, and drained raspberries
2 tablespoons tapioca

½ cup unsweetened pineapple juice concentrate (Minute Maid)

1. Puree berries in a blender and press through a strainer to remove seeds.

2. Combine all ingredients in a small saucepan and allow to sit for 5 minutes.

3. Place saucepan over medium heat and bring mixture to a boil, stirring constantly. Continue boiling and stirring for 1 minute, then remove pan from heat and allow mixture to cool for 20 minutes before stirring well and spooning into small bowls or parfait glasses.

4. Chill in refrigerator for 3 hours before serving.

Yield: 4 servings

PER SERVING

Calories: 113
Protein: 1.1 g
Fat: 3.4 g
Carbohydrate: 27.1 g

Sodium: 12.6 mg
Diabetic exchanges
   Fruit: 2

Apple or Pear Pudding Sauce

3 apples or pears, peeled, cored, and sliced
⅓ cup unsweetened pineapple juice concentrate (Minute Maid) or unsweetened apple juice concentrate (any brand)
Generous ½ teaspoon cinnamon

¾ cup water (if necessary, add ⅛ cup additional water while mixture is cooking to retain puddinglike consistency)
1 tablespoon plus 1 teaspoon all-purpose flour

1. In a medium-sized saucepan, combine fruit, concentrate, cinnamon, and water. Place saucepan over medium heat and bring mixture to a boil. Reduce heat and simmer until tender—about 45 minutes—stirring occasionally. Remove pan from heat, mash mixture, and allow it to cool slightly.

2. Add flour, return saucepan to medium heat, and bring mixture to a boil, stirring constantly. Continue to cook and stir at a light boil for 2 to 3 minutes. Remove pan from heat and allow mixture to cool.

3. Serve plain or pour cooled mixture into a No-Bake Graham-Cracker Crust (page 61) or use as a topping for Apple-Cinnamon or Pear-Cinnamon Rolls (page 20). Refrigerate or freeze in an airtight container.

Yield: 4 servings or enough topping for 27 rolls

PER SERVING

Calories: 116
Protein: 0.8 g
Fat: 0.7 g
Carbohydrate: 28.8 g

Sodium: 9.3 mg
Diabetic exchanges
　Fruit: 2

Quick Apple or Pear Pudding

4 cups peeled, cored, and sliced apple or
   pear
⅓ cup unsweetened pineapple juice
   concentrate (Minute Maid) or
   unsweetened apple juice concentrate
   (any brand)

½ teaspoon cinnamon
2 tablespoons plus ½ teaspoon
   arrowroot or cornstarch
Chopped nuts or unsweetened coconut
   (optional)

1. Puree fruit and concentrate in blender.
2. In a medium-sized saucepan, combine fruit mixture and cinnamon. Place saucepan over medium heat and bring mixture to a boil. Partially cover to allow steam to escape, reduce heat, and simmer for 10 minutes, stirring occasionally. Be careful to avoid splatters.
3. Remove pan from heat and let mixture cool.
4. When mixture is cool, add arrowroot (or cornstarch), place saucepan over medium heat, and stir constantly. Arrowroot will thicken the mixture before it reaches the boiling point. (Cornstarch will thicken it 1 to 2 minutes after it reaches the boiling point.)
5. When mixture reaches desired pudding consistency, remove pan from heat and let cool for 15 minutes. Stir mixture, pour into serving bowls, cover, and refrigerate until ready to serve. Serve plain or topped with chopped nuts or moistened unsweetened coconut, if desired. (Coconut can be premoistened with a little water and vegetable oil. Just mix and let coconut soak up moisture for a few minutes before sprinkling on pudding.) If you are going to stir coconut into the pudding, do not moisten the coconut.

Yield: 4 servings

PER SERVING

Calories: 122
Protein: 0.6 g
Fat: 0.4 g
Carbohydrate: 29.4 g

Sodium: 9.4 mg
Diabetic exchanges
  Fruit: 2

Apple or Pear or Peach Sauce

4 pieces fruit (apples, pears, or
   peaches), peeled, cored, and sliced
Scant ½ teaspoon cinnamon
½ cup unsweetened pineapple juice
   concentrate (Minute Maid) or
   unsweetened apple juice concentrate
   (any brand)

½ cup water (if necessary, add ⅛ to ¼
   cup additional water while mixture is
   cooking to retain puddinglike
   consistency)

1. In a medium-sized saucepan, combine all ingredients. Place saucepan over medium heat and bring mixture to a boil. Reduce heat and simmer for 45 minutes, stirring occasionally, until fruit is soft and cooked through.

2. Remove pan from heat and allow mixture to cool for 20 minutes.

3. With a fork or potato masher, mash fruit to sauce consistency, pour into container, and refrigerate until ready to use.

Yield: 4 servings

PER SERVING (USING APPLES FOR FRUIT)

Calories: 148
Protein: 0.8 g
Fat: 0.5 g
Carbohydrate: 37.4 g

Sodium: 13.7 mg
Diabetic exchanges
   Fruit: 2½

Chocolate Pudding

No Dairy
No Corn

⅓ cup water	¼ cup date sugar
1 ounce (1 square) Baker's Unsweetened All-Natural Chocolate	1¾ cups water
	3 tablespoons arrowroot
1 teaspoon vegetable oil	

1. In a medium-sized saucepan over medium heat and stirring constantly, melt together water, chocolate, and oil.

2. Turn heat to medium-high, add date sugar, and cook, stirring, until mixture starts to boil. Reduce heat to medium and continue cooking for 2 to 2½ minutes.

3. Remove saucepan from heat and stir in 1¾ cups water. Add arrowroot and stir well.

4. Pour mixture into blender and blend at high speed for 30 seconds.

5. Pour mixture back into saucepan. Place over medium-high heat, stirring constantly, until mixture starts to thicken. Reduce heat to medium and continue to cook and stir for about 1 to 1½ minutes, until mixture is desired pudding consistency.

6. Remove pan from heat and pour mixture into large bowl to cool. As it cools, pudding will form a skin on top. After 15 minutes of cooling, stir well and let cool another 15 to 20 minutes. Stir well again, pour pudding into four serving bowls, and refrigerate until ready to serve. If pudding collects moisture while in refrigerator, simply pour off moisture and stir again before serving.

Yield: 4 servings or enough pie filling for one 9-inch pie

VARIATION: This pudding can also be used as a pie filling (pour cooled pudding into No-Bake Graham-Cracker Crust—page 61—and refrigerate before serving) or for frozen Chocolate Pudding Pops (page 146).

PER SERVING

Calories: 90	*Sodium:* 0.4 mg
Protein: 4.2 g	*Diabetic exchanges*
Fat: 4.8 g	*Bread:* ¾
Carbohydrate: 13.1 g	*Fat:* 1

Fast-and-Easy Fruit Sauce

3 cups peeled and sliced fruit of choice
  (apple, pear, peach)
⅓ cup unsweetened pineapple juice
  concentrate (Minute Maid) or
  unsweetened apple juice concentrate
  (any brand)

Scant ½ teaspoon cinnamon
Chopped nuts or unsweetened coconut
  (optional)

1. Puree fruit and concentrate in blender.

2. In a medium-sized saucepan, combine fruit mixture and cinnamon. Place saucepan over medium heat and bring to a boil. Partially cover to allow steam to escape, reduce heat, and simmer for 10 minutes, stirring occasionally. Be careful to avoid splatters.

3. Remove pan from heat and let mixture cool. Serve immediately, plain or topped with chopped nuts or moistened unsweetened coconut (coconut can be premoistened with a little water and vegetable oil; just mix and let coconut soak up moisture for a few minutes before sprinkling on pudding). If you are going to stir coconut into the sauce, do not moisten the coconut. Pour sauce into container, cover, and refrigerate if not serving immediately.

Yield: 4 servings

PER SERVING (USING ONE CUP EACH OF APPLE, PEAR, AND PEACH)

Calories: 97
Protein: 0.8 g
Fat: 1.2 g
Carbohydrate: 24.5 g

Sodium: 9.1 mg
Diabetic exchanges
  Fruit: 1½

Pineapple-Nut Pudding

One 20-ounce can unsweetened
 pineapple chunks (use Dole if you are
 allergic to phenol)
2 tablespoons unsweetened pineapple
 juice concentrate (Minute Maid)
1 tablespoon plus 1 teaspoon arrowroot
 or cornstarch

2 tablespoons *dry* unsweetened coconut,
 sesame seeds, or poppy seeds
⅛ teaspoon cinnamon
2 tablespoons chopped pecans

1. Measure ¾ cup pineapple chunks, drain, reserving juice, and pat dry. Set aside.

2. Place remaining pineapple chunks and all the juice from the can in blender. Add pineapple juice concentrate and blend.

3. In a medium-sized saucepan, combine pineapple puree and arrowroot (or cornstarch). Place saucepan over medium heat and stir constantly. Arrowroot will thicken the mixture before it reaches the boiling point. (Cornstarch will thicken it 1 to 2 minutes after it reaches the boiling point.)

4. When mixture reaches desired pudding consistency, remove from heat, add ¾ cup dry pineapple chunks, coconut, cinnamon, and pecans. Stir, cool for 20 minutes, stir again, and pour into four small bowls. Cover and refrigerate until ready to serve.

Yield: 4 servings

PER SERVING

Calories: 147
Protein: 0.8 g
Fat: 3.4 g
Carbohydrate: 29.7 g

Sodium: 16.3 mg
Diabetic exchanges
 Fat: ½
 Fruit: 2

Quick Peach Pudding

4 cups peeled, pitted, and chopped
  peaches
½ cup unsweetened pineapple juice
  concentrate (Minute Maid) or
  unsweetened apple juice concentrate
  (any brand)

½ teaspoon cinnamon
4 tablespoons arrowroot or cornstarch
Chopped nuts or unsweetened coconut
  (optional)

1. Puree peaches and concentrate in blender.

2. In a medium-sized saucepan, combine fruit mixture and cinnamon. Place saucepan over medium heat and bring to a boil. Partially cover to allow steam to escape, reduce heat, and simmer for 10 minutes, stirring occasionally. Be careful to avoid splatters.

3. Remove pan from heat and let mixture cool.

4. When mixture is cool, add arrowroot (or cornstarch), place saucepan over medium heat, and stir constantly. Arrowroot will thicken the mixture before it reaches the boiling point. (Cornstarch will thicken it 1 to 2 minutes after it reaches the boiling point.)

5. When mixture reaches desired pudding consistency, remove pan from heat and let mixture cool for 15 minutes. Stir mixture, pour into serving bowls, cover, and refrigerate until ready to serve. Serve plain or top with chopped nuts or moistened unsweetened coconut (coconut can be premoistened with a little water and vegetable oil; just mix and let coconut absorb moisture for a few minutes before sprinkling on pudding). If you are going to stir coconut into the pudding, do not moisten the coconut.

Yield: 4 servings

PER SERVING

Calories: 167
Protein: 1.7 g
Fat: 0.2 g
Carbohydrate: 42.0 g

Sodium: 13.9 mg
Diabetic exchanges
  Fruit: 2¾

COOKIES, BARS, AND CANDIES

Yes, it's possible to create great-tasting candies and cookies without using refined sugar or honey. By substituting fruit concentrates, date sugar, or brown-rice syrup, you can turn out sweet treats that the whole family will enjoy. Brown-rice syrup can be found in most health-food stores; one brand I use is Westbrae Natural Brown Rice Syrup; another brand is Sweet Dreams Brown Rice Syrup made by Lundberg.

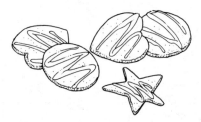

Coco-Nut Fudge Balls

1½ cups date sugar
¼ cup unsweetened grape juice
    concentrate (any brand)
¼ cup unsweetened pineapple juice
    concentrate (Minute Maid)
2 tablespoons vegetable oil
2 ounces (2 squares) Baker's
    Unsweetened All-Natural Chocolate

5 tablespoons water
2 egg whites
¾ cup chopped nuts
Garnish: ⅓ to ⅔ cup chopped nuts
    and/or ⅓ to ⅔ cup unsweetened
    coconut, premoistened with 1¼
    teaspoons water and 1¼ teaspoons
    vegetable oil

1. In a medium-sized saucepan, combine all ingredients except egg whites, nuts, and garnish. Place saucepan over medium heat and cook for 2 minutes, stirring constantly so mixture will not burn. Remove saucepan from heat and let mixture cool for 3 to 5 minutes.

2. Beat in egg whites, return saucepan to medium heat, and cook, stirring, until mixture is thick. Remove saucepan from heat and stir in ¾ cup chopped nuts.

3. Pour mixture into an 8- by 8- by 2-inch pan and freeze for 1 hour.

4. Remove pan from freezer. Using your fingers, place a small portion of the mixture in the palm of your hand and roll into a 1-inch ball. Repeat to form 12 balls.

5. Roll balls in garnish. Freeze in airtight container until ready to serve (fudge tastes best frozen). Aging in the freezer for 2 to 3 weeks enhances the flavor of the fudge.

Yield: 12 balls

PER BALL (USING PECANS FOR CHOPPED NUTS)

Calories: 188
Protein: 2.5 g
Fat: 12.0 g
Carbohydrate: 20.6 g

Sodium: 10.8 mg
Diabetic exchanges
    Fat: 2⅓
    Fruit: 1⅓

Space Balls

⅓ cup chopped (cut with scissors) and packed dates

⅓ cup *dry* unsweetened coconut

¼ cup packed raisins

⅓ cup chopped (cut with scissors) and packed dried Calimyrna figs

⅓ cup chopped pecans

2 tablespoons rice syrup (Westbrae Natural Brown Rice Syrup)

Generous ½ cup unsweetened coconut, premoistened with 1½ teaspoons water and 1½ teaspoons vegetable oil

1. In a large bowl, stir together all ingredients except rice syrup and premoistened coconut.

2. Stir in rice syrup 1 tablespoon at a time.

3. Roll mixture into 8 balls, shaping firmly.

4. Roll balls in premoistened coconut. To store, place balls in an airtight container and refrigerate or freeze.

Yield: 8 balls

PER BALL

Calories: 132
Protein: 1.2 g
Fat: 7.2 g
Carbohydrate: 18.1 g

Sodium: 3.9 mg
Diabetic exchanges
 Fat: 1½
 Fruit: 1¼

Chocolate-Dipped Pecan Dates

20 large pitted dates
Approximately ¼ cup pecan pieces
¼ cup water
2 ounces (2 squares) Baker's All-Natural Unsweetened Chocolate

1 tablespoon vegetable oil
½ cup plus 2 tablespoons date sugar
¼ cup rice syrup (Westbrae Natural Brown Rice Syrup)

1. Stuff dates with pecan pieces, enlarging ends of dates with a knife if necessary.

2. In a medium-sized saucepan, combine water, chocolate, and oil. Place saucepan over medium heat until chocolate is melted, stirring constantly.

3. Add date sugar to melted chocolate mixture and continue stirring over medium heat for 1 minute.

4. Add rice syrup and continue stirring over medium heat until mixture starts to become gooey—1 to 2 minutes. Remove saucepan from heat and allow mixture to cool for 1 to 2 minutes.

5. Using a large metal spoon, dip each date in chocolate mixture until completely coated, then place on waxed paper.

6. When all dates are coated, if you have chocolate left over in saucepan, spoon excess evenly over cooling dates. As the mixture cools, the chocolate will become less gooey. Roll each one between your palms until chocolate is smooth and date is completely covered.

7. Wrap each date in a small piece of plastic wrap, twisting ends of wrap. Place wrapped dates in large plastic bag and freeze until ready to serve. Let thaw 10 to 15 minutes before serving.

Yield: 20 dates

PER DATE

Calories: 82
Protein: 0.9 g
Fat: 4.1 g
Carbohydrate: 12.1 g

Sodium: 0.6 mg
Diabetic exchanges
Fat: ¾
Fruit: ¾

Banana-Coconut Bars

⅓ cup vegetable oil

Generous 1 cup mashed banana

4 egg whites *or* 2 extralarge eggs

½ cup water or milk

1¾ cups all-purpose flour

1 cup unsweetened coconut,
  premoistened with 2½ to 2¾
  teaspoons water and 2½ to 2¾
  teaspoons vegetable oil

1 teaspoon baking soda

2¼ teaspoons baking powder

½ cup unsweetened coconut,
  premoistened with 1¼ to 1½
  teaspoons water and 1¼ to 1½
  teaspoons vegetable oil (for topping)

1. Preheat oven to 350°F. Oil and flour a 13- by 9- by 2-inch baking pan.

2. Combine all ingredients except baking soda, baking powder, and ½ cup coconut in a large bowl and beat well by hand.

3. Stir in baking soda and baking powder quickly, and then mix (28 to 30 beats); immediately pour mixture into prepared baking pan.

4. Quickly sprinkle ½ cup coconut on batter and bake 20 to 22 minutes or until a toothpick inserted in center comes out clean.

5. Remove pan from oven and let mixture cool in pan. Cut into 15 bars. To store, place cooled bars in an airtight container and refrigerate or freeze.

Yield: 15 bars

PER BAR

Calories: 152

Protein: 2.7 g

Fat: 9.0 g

Carbohydrate: 15.5 g

Sodium: 119.2 mg

Diabetic exchanges

  Bread: 1

  Fat: 1¾

120

Banana-Coconut Bars

No Egg

⅓ cup vegetable oil
Generous 1 cup mashed banana
½ cup water
1¾ cups all-purpose flour
¼ cup water
1 tablespoon egg replacer (Ener-G
  brand)
1 cup unsweetened coconut,
  premoistened with 1 tablespoon
  water and 1 tablespoon vegetable oil

1 teaspoon baking soda
2½ teaspoons baking powder
½ cup unsweetened coconut,
  premoistened with 1½ teaspoons
  water and 1½ teaspoons vegetable oil
  (for topping)

1. Preheat oven to 350°F. Oil and flour a 13- by 9- by 2-inch baking pan.

2. In a large bowl, combine ⅓ cup oil, banana, and water; beat by hand for 45 seconds. Add flour and beat for 2 minutes.

3. In a small bowl, and using a hand-operated mechanical beater, beat together water and egg replacer until bubbles form (mixture should not be thick or stiff). Pour egg-replacer mixture into banana mixture and stir for 20 seconds by hand. Stir in 1 cup of premoistened coconut. Stir in baking soda and baking powder quickly, and then mix (28 to 30 beats); immediately pour mixture into prepared baking pan. Sprinkle remaining ½ cup coconut evenly over batter.

4. Bake about 23 minutes or until a toothpick inserted in center comes out clean.

5. Remove pan from oven and let mixture cool in pan. Cut into 15 bars. To store, place cooled bars in an airtight container and refrigerate or freeze.

Yield: 15 bars

PER BAR

Calories: 143
Protein: 1.9 g
Fat: 8.3 g
Carbohydrate: 15.6 g

Sodium: 110.9 mg
Diabetic exchanges
  Bread: 1
  Fat: 1½

Banana-Oat-Cinnamon Bars

2 cups oat flour
½ cup rolled oats
¼ teaspoon salt
3½ teaspoons baking powder
1 teaspoon baking soda
½ teaspoon cinnamon

½ teaspoon nutmeg
Generous ¾ cup mashed banana
4 tablespoons oat flour
3 tablespoons vegetable oil
4 tablespoons water

1. Preheat oven to 350°F. Oil a 9- by 9- by 2-inch baking pan.

2. In a large bowl and using a fork, stir together oat flour, rolled oats, salt, baking powder, baking soda, cinnamon, and nutmeg.

3. In a medium-sized bowl, combine banana, 4 tablespoons oat flour, oil, and water. Beat with a hand-operated mechanical beater until well mixed.

4. Add banana mixture to oat-flour mixture and stir quickly (28 to 30 beats); immediately pour batter into prepared pan.

5. Bake 30 to 35 minutes or until knife inserted into center comes out clean.

6. Remove pan from oven and let mixture cool in pan. Cut into 9 bars. To store, place cooled bars in an airtight container and refrigerate or freeze.

Yield: 9 bars

PER BAR

Calories: 183
Protein: 5.3 g
Fat: 6.4 g
Carbohydrate: 27.9 g

Sodium: 253.0 mg
Diabetic exchanges
 Bread: 1¾
 Fat: 1¼

Banana-Oat-Coconut Bars

1 cup oat flour

1 cup Ener-G brand oat mix (see *Note*)

½ cup unsweetened coconut, premoistened with 1¼ teaspoons water and 1¼ teaspoons vegetable oil

¼ teaspoon salt

3½ teaspoons baking powder

1 teaspoon baking soda

½ teaspoon cinnamon

¼ teaspoon nutmeg

Generous 1 cup mashed banana

4 tablespoons oat flour

3 tablespoons vegetable oil

4 tablespoons water

¼ cup unsweetened coconut, premoistened with ¾ teaspoon water and ¾ teaspoon vegetable oil (for topping)

1. Preheat oven to 350°F. Oil a 9- by 9- by 2-inch baking pan.

2. In a large bowl and using a fork, stir together the 1 cup oat flour, 1 cup oat mix, ½ cup coconut, salt, baking powder, baking soda, cinnamon, and nutmeg.

3. In a medium-sized bowl, combine banana, 4 tablespoons oat flour, oil, and water. Beat with a hand-operated mechanical beater until well mixed.

4. Add banana mixture to oat-flour mixture and stir quickly (28 to 30 beats). Pour batter quickly into prepared pan and sprinkle with ¼ cup premoistened coconut.

5. Bake 30 to 35 minutes or until knife inserted in center comes out clean.

6. Remove pan from oven and cool on a wire rack. Cut into 9 bars. To store, place cooled bars in an airtight container and refrigerate or freeze.

Yield: 9 bars

PER BAR

Calories: 204

Protein: 4.7 g

Fat: 10.2 g

Carbohydrate: 25.4 g

Sodium: 276.0 mg

Diabetic exchanges

 Bread: 1½

 Fat: 2

Note: You may substitute 1 cup regular oat flour for 1 cup Ener-G brand oat mix, in which case you must add an additional ½ teaspoon baking powder.

Date Bars

1 cup raisins

¾ cup plus 2 tablespoons date sugar

½ cup crushed and drained
    unsweetened pineapple (use Dole if
    you are allergic to phenol)

½ cup pineapple juice from can

½ cup unsweetened pineapple juice
    concentrate (Minute Maid)

¼ cup water

⅓ cup plus 1 tablespoon vegetable oil

1½ cups plus 2 tablespoons all-purpose
    flour

4 egg whites *or* 2 extralarge eggs

¼ cup unsweetened coconut,
    premoistened with ½ to ¾ teaspoon
    water and ½ to ¾ teaspoon vegetable
    oil

¾ cup chopped nuts

1 teaspoon cinnamon

¼ teaspoon nutmeg

1¼ teaspoons baking soda

1. Preheat oven to 350°F. Oil and flour a 13- by 9- by 2-inch baking pan.

2. In a medium-sized saucepan, combine raisins, date sugar, pineapple, pineapple juice, pineapple juice concentrate, and water. Place saucepan over medium heat, bring mixture to a boil, and boil for 3 minutes, stirring frequently.

3. Remove saucepan from heat, add oil, stir, and let cool.

4. In a medium-sized bowl, stir together flour, eggs, coconut, chopped nuts, cinnamon, and nutmeg.

5. Add cooled pineapple mixture to flour mixture and stir well. Stir in baking soda quickly, and then mix (28 to 30 beats); immediately spoon batter into prepared pan.

6. Bake 30 minutes or until bars pull away slightly from sides of pan and feel firm to the touch.

7. Remove pan from oven and let mixture cool in pan. Slice into bars. To store, place cooled bars in an airtight container and refrigerate or freeze.

Yield: 15 bars

PER BAR (USING PECANS FOR CHOPPED NUTS)

Calories: 226

Protein: 3.3 g

Fat: 10.4 g

Carbohydrate: 30.9 g

Sodium: 87.6 mg

Diabetic exchanges

Bread: 1

Fat: 2

Fruit: 1

Super-Sweet Date Bars

1 cup raisins

¾ cup plus 2 tablespoons date sugar

½ cup crushed and drained unsweetened pineapple (use Dole if you are allergic to phenol)

2 teaspoons pineapple juice from can

1¼ cups unsweetened pineapple juice concentrate (Minute Maid)

⅓ cup plus 1 tablespoon vegetable oil

1½ cups plus 2 tablespoons all-purpose flour

4 egg whites *or* 2 extralarge eggs, beaten

¼ cup unsweetened coconut, premoistened with ½ to ¾ teaspoon water and ½ to ¾ teaspoon vegetable oil

¾ cup chopped nuts

1 teaspoon cinnamon

¼ teaspoon nutmeg

1½ teaspoons baking soda

1. Preheat oven to 350°F. Oil and flour a 13- by 9- by 2-inch baking pan.

2. In a medium-sized saucepan, combine raisins, date sugar, pineapple, pineapple juice, and pineapple juice concentrate. Place saucepan over medium heat, bring mixture to a boil, and boil for 3 minutes, stirring frequently.

3. Remove saucepan from heat, add oil, stir, and let cool.

4. In a medium-sized bowl, stir together flour, eggs, coconut, chopped nuts, cinnamon, and nutmeg.

5. Add cooled pineapple mixture to flour mixture and stir well for 2 minutes. Stir in baking soda quickly and then mix (28 to 30 beats); immediately pour batter into prepared pan.

6. Bake about 34 minutes or until bars pull away slightly from sides of pan and feel firm to the touch.

7. Remove pan from oven and let mixture cool in pan. Slice into bars. To store, place cooled bars in an airtight container and refrigerate or freeze.

Yield: 15 bars

PER BAR (USING PECANS FOR CHOPPED NUTS)

Calories: 248

Protein: 3.6 g

Fat: 10.4 g

Carbohydrate: 34.7 g

Sodium: 105.9 mg

Diabetic exchanges

Bread: 1

Fat: 2

Fruit: 1⅓

Fig-Nut Bars

No Egg

¼ cup vegetable oil

¼ cup unsweetened apple juice concentrate (any brand)

½ cup plus 2 tablespoons plus ½ teaspoon water

1½ teaspoons pure potato-starch flour

1½ cups plus 1 tablespoon all-purpose flour

½ cup chopped (cut with scissors) and packed dried Calimyrna figs

10 chopped (cut with scissors) dried Black Mission figs

⅓ cup chopped pecans

2 tablespoons sesame seeds

2 tablespoons water

1½ teaspoons egg replacer (Ener-G brand)

1 teaspoon baking soda

2½ teaspoons baking powder

¼ cup chopped pecans (for topping)

1. Preheat oven to 350°F. Oil and flour a 9- by 9- by 2-inch baking pan.

2. In a large bowl, stir together oil, concentrate, water, and potato-starch flour. Add all-purpose flour and beat for 2 minutes by hand. Add Calimyrna and Black Mission figs, ⅓ cup pecans, and sesame seeds, and beat for 2 minutes by hand.

3. In a small bowl, and using a hand-operated mechanical beater, beat together water and egg replacer until bubbles form (mixture should not be thick or stiff). Pour egg-replacer mixture into fig mixture and stir for 20 seconds by hand. Stir in baking soda and baking powder quickly, and then mix (28 to 30 beats); immediately pour mixture into prepared baking pan. Quickly sprinkle ¼ cup chopped pecans evenly over top.

4. Bake 35 minutes or until a cake tester inserted in center comes out clean.

5. Remove pan from oven and cool on a wire rack. Cut into bars. To store, place cooled bars in an airtight container and refrigerate or freeze.

Yield: 9 bars

PER BAR

Calories: 281
Protein: 4.1 g
Fat: 12.7 g
Carbohydrate: 39.3 g
Sodium: 189.2 mg

Diabetic exchanges
  Bread: 1½
  Fat: 2½
  Fruit: 1

126

Granola Bars

2½ cups rolled oats
¼ cup sesame seeds
⅛ cup raw hulled sunflower seeds
½ cup raw wheat germ
½ cup unsweetened coconut, premoistened with 1½ teaspoons water and 1½ teaspoons vegetable oil
¾ cup chopped pecans

1 cup chopped (cut with scissors) and packed raisins, dates, and dried figs (any combination)
2 tablespoons vegetable oil
Generous ¾ cup rice syrup (Sweet Dreams Brown Rice Syrup by Lundberg)

1. Preheat oven to 275°F. Oil a 15- by 10- by ½-inch baking pan.

2. In a large bowl, mix together all ingredients with a fork. Pour into prepared baking pan. Dampen hands with water and press down firmly on the dough, leaving a 10- by 1-inch rectangle of pan bottom uncovered so that you can use a spatula to test the bottom of the mixture for doneness.

3. Bake about 31 minutes or until bottoms of bars show just a *hint* of color change. (Bars will get crisper as they cool so don't let bottom become golden.)

4. Remove pan from oven and place on wire rack to cool for 10 to 15 minutes. Use a knife to cut into bars. To store, place cooled bars in an airtight container and refrigerate or freeze.

Yield: 18 bars

PER BAR (USING ONLY RAISINS FOR CHOPPED FRUIT)

Calories: 180
Protein: 4.4 g
Fat: 8.7 g
Carbohydrate: 23.6 g
Sodium: 3.6 mg

Diabetic exchanges
  Bread: 1
  Fat: 1½
  Fruit: ½

Dried-Fruit Granola Bars

No Oatmeal or Wheat

½ cup chopped (cut with scissors) and packed dried Calimyrna figs

½ cup chopped (cut with scissors) and packed dates

½ cup packed raisins

½ cup chopped (cut with scissors) and packed prunes

¼ cup sesame seeds

1½ cups chopped pecans

¼ cup raw, hulled sunflower seeds

½ cup unsweetened coconut, premoistened with 1 tablespoon water and 1 tablespoon vegetable oil

¼ cup brown-rice syrup (Westbrae Natural Brown Rice Syrup)

1. Preheat oven to 275°F. Oil an 8- by 8- by 2-inch baking pan.

2. In a large bowl, combine all ingredients. Pour into prepared baking pan. Dampen hands with water and press down firmly on dough.

3. Bake for 28 minutes or until bars become nearly dry and less sticky to the touch. (Bars will get firmer as they cool, so be careful not to overcook.)

4. Remove pan from oven and place on a wire rack to cool for 20 minutes. With a down-up motion, use a spatula to cut into 9 bars. Leave bars in pan and refrigerate, uncovered, until completely cooled. To serve, remove bars with a spatula and place on a serving plate. To store, place cooled bars in an airtight container and refrigerate or freeze.

Yield: 9 bars

PER BAR

Calories: 321

Protein: 4.3 g

Fat: 20.7 g

Carbohydrate: 34.8 g

Sodium: 5.8 mg

Diabetic exchanges

  Fat: 4

  Fruit: 2¼

Cashew Butter or Peanut Butter Cookies

½ cup vegetable shortening or lard

2 teaspoons vegetable oil

½ cup cashew butter or peanut butter
(all-natural, unsweetened; if using
cashew butter, add an additional ½
teaspoon oil)

1 cup date sugar

2 egg whites *or* 1 extralarge egg, beaten

¼ cup plus 1 tablespoon water

1¼ cups all-purpose flour

¼ teaspoon salt

1¼ teaspoons baking soda

½ teaspoon baking powder

1. Preheat oven to 350°F. Grease two cookie sheets with vegetable shortening or oil.

2. In a large bowl, combine all ingredients except baking soda and baking powder and beat well by hand.

3. Add baking soda and baking powder and mix quickly but well.

4. Quickly form mixture into about 30 small balls, place on prepared cookie sheets, and flatten slightly with a fork.

5. Bake 10 to 12 minutes or until cookies are slightly golden around edges. Rotate cookie sheets at the halfway point to achieve even baking. Remove cookie sheets from oven, remove cookies from sheets, and place on a countertop to cool. To store, place cooled cookies in an airtight container and refrigerate or freeze.

Yield: 30 cookies

PER COOKIE

Calories: 94

Protein: 1.6 g

Fat: 6.0 g

Carbohydrate: 8.2 g

Sodium: 59.8 mg

Diabetic exchanges

   Bread: ½

   Fat: 1¼

Cashew Butter–Granola Cookies

No Cereal

½ cup plus 3 tablespoons cashew butter
1 cup chopped cashews
¼ cup sesame seeds
¼ cup raw, hulled sunflower seeds
¾ cup combination of chopped (cut with scissors) and packed dried Black Mission figs and chopped (cut with scissors) and packed dried Calimyrna figs

¾ cup chopped (cut with scissors) and packed dates
½ cup packed raisins
½ cup unsweetened coconut, premoistened with 1 tablespoon water and 1 tablespoon vegetable oil

1. Preheat oven to 275°F. Oil two 9- by 9- by 1½-inch baking pans (baking pans will hold in moisture better than cookie sheets).

2. In a large bowl, stir together all ingredients.

3. Using your hands, roll mixture into 20 balls. Flatten balls by hand and place in prepared pans.

4. Bake 18 to 20 minutes or until cookies feel dry to the touch (they will not turn golden brown).

5. Remove pan from oven and remove cookies to a countertop until completely cool. To store, place cooled cookies in an airtight container and refrigerate or freeze.

Yield: 20 cookies

PER COOKIE (USING UNSALTED CASHEWS)

Calories: 174
Protein: 3.8 g
Fat: 10.8 g
Carbohydrate: 17.3 g

Sodium: 3.2 mg
Diabetic exchanges
  Fat: 2
  Fruit: 1¼

Mike's Fig Cookies

This recipe was created by my son, Michael. Try adding seeds, nuts, coconut, dates, or raisins for extra variety.

2 heaping cups chopped (cut with scissors) and packed dried Black Mission figs
½ cup water
½ cup vegetable oil

4 egg whites *or* 2 extralarge eggs
½ teaspoon salt
3 cups rolled oats
1½ teaspoons baking soda

1. Preheat oven to 375°F. Oil two large cookie sheets.

2. In a large bowl, combine chopped figs, water, oil, and eggs. Use a strong spoon to break up and mash the figs into a soupy pulp that is free of major lumps. (A blender or food processor will not work because the figs get caught in the blades.)

3. Add salt and oats to fig mixture and mix well. Add baking soda and mix quickly but well.

4. Quickly shape dough into about 28 small balls with your hands. Flatten balls slightly and place on prepared cookie sheets.

5. Bake 7 minutes at 375°F, reduce oven temperature to 350°F, and continue baking for another 7 to 8 minutes or until cookies are slightly golden around edges. Rotate cookie sheets at the halfway point to achieve even baking.

6. Remove cookie sheets from oven; remove cookies from sheets and place on a countertop until completely cool. To store, place cooled cookies in an airtight container and refrigerate or freeze.

Yield: 28 cookies

PER COOKIE

Calories: 103
Protein: 2.4 g
Fat: 4.7 g
Carbohydrate: 14.5 g
Sodium: 87.4 mg

Diabetic exchanges
  Bread: ½
  Fat: 1
  Fruit: ½

Fruit Cookies

1¼ cups unsweetened pineapple/orange juice concentrate (Minute Maid)

⅓ cup packed raisins

Generous ½ cup chopped (cut with scissors) and packed dried Calimyrna figs

Generous ½ cup crushed unsweetened banana chips

4 egg whites *or* 2 extralarge eggs

⅓ cup vegetable oil

½ teaspoon cinnamon

3 cups all-purpose flour

2 teaspoons baking soda

1. Preheat oven to 350°F. Oil two large cookie sheets.

2. In a large bowl, stir together concentrate, raisins, figs, banana chips, eggs, oil, and cinnamon.

3. Add flour and mix well.

4. Add baking soda and mix quickly but well.

5. Quickly drop batter by tablespoonfuls onto prepared cookie sheets.

6. Bake 8 to 9 minutes or until cookies are slightly golden around edges. Rotate cookie sheets at the halfway point to achieve even baking.

7. Remove pans from oven; remove cookies from pans and place on a countertop until completely cool. To store, place cookies in an airtight container and refrigerate or freeze.

Yield: 40 cookies

PER COOKIE

Calories: 86
Protein: 1.6 g
Fat: 2.5 g
Carbohydrate: 14.3 g
Sodium: 50 mg

Diabetic exchanges
  Bread: ½
  Fat: ½
  Fruit: ½

Graham-Cracker Cookie Cutouts

These cookies can be cut into any desired shape. They can also be crumbled after baking and used as a base for No-Bake Graham-Cracker Crust (page 61).

¾ cup vegetable shortening
1¼ cups date sugar
¼ cup water
4 egg whites *or* 2 extralarge eggs
2 tablespoons unsweetened pineapple juice concentrate (Minute Maid)

2¾ cups all-purpose flour
½ teaspoon salt
1¼ teaspoons baking soda
¾ teaspoon baking powder
Chocolate-Date Frosting (page 43)

1. Preheat oven to 350°F. Oil two large cookie sheets.

2. In a large bowl, combine shortening, date sugar, and water and beat by hand until fluffy.

3. Add eggs and pineapple juice concentrate and stir well.

4. In a medium-sized bowl, combine flour, salt, baking soda, and baking powder, and stir until well mixed.

5. Gradually add flour mixture to shortening mixture, stirring well after each addition.

6. Place dough on a lightly floured surface and roll out to ¼-inch thickness. Cut into cookie shapes using cookie cutters. Place cut-out dough on prepared cookie sheets.

7. Bake 11 to 12 minutes or until cookies are golden around edges. Rotate cookie sheets at halfway point to achieve even baking.

8. Remove pans from oven; remove cookies from pans and place on a countertop until completely cool.

9. Spread Chocolate Date Frosting on cooled cookies. Allow frosting to dry before serving or storing in an airtight container in refrigerator or freezer.

Yield: 18 cookies

PER COOKIE WITHOUT FROSTING

Calories: 178
Protein: 3.0 g
Fat: 8.4 g
Carbohydrate: 22.0 g
Sodium: 141.7 mg

Diabetic exchanges
  Bread: 1
  Fat: 1½
  Fruit: ½

Oatmeal/Coconut-Date Cookies

¾ cup date sugar

5 tablespoons vegetable oil

2 egg whites *or* 1 extralarge egg

¼ cup water

Generous 1½ cups rolled oats

½ cup all-purpose flour

½ teaspoon salt

¼ cup unsweetened coconut, premoistened with 1 teaspoon water and 1 teaspoon vegetable oil

⅓ cup chopped (cut with scissors) and packed dried figs, premixed with 1½ teaspoons all-purpose flour

⅓ cup packed raisins

½ cup chopped (cut with scissors) and packed dates, premixed with 1½ teaspoons all-purpose flour

1 teaspoon baking soda

1. Preheat oven to 325°F. Oil two large cookie sheets.

2. In a medium-sized bowl, beat together date sugar, oil, egg, and water.

3. In a large bowl, stir together oats, flour, salt, coconut, figs, raisins, dates, and baking soda.

4. Pour oat mixture a little at a time into egg-and-water mixture and stir well.

5. Quickly drop batter by tablespoonfuls on prepared cookie sheets. Flatten cookies slightly with a fork.

6. Bake 13 to 14 minutes or until cookies are slightly golden around edges. Rotate cookie sheets at the halfway point to achieve even baking.

7. Remove pans from oven; remove cookies from pans and place on a countertop until completely cool. To store, place cooled cookies in an airtight container and refrigerate or freeze.

Yield: 28 cookies

PER COOKIE

Calories: 82
Protein: 1.6 g
Fat: 3.3 g
Carbohydrate: 12.6 g
Sodium: 68.5 mg

Diabetic exchanges
  Bread: ½
  Fat: ½
  Fruit: ½

Crispy Rice-Date Bars
(or Caramel "Popcorn")

4 rice cakes, crumbled (use any brand; omit additional salt if using salted rice cakes)

Scant ¼ teaspoon sea salt

Generous ¼ teaspoon allspice

13 finely chopped (cut with scissors) dates

3 tablespoons plus 1½ teaspoons rice syrup (Sweet Dreams Brown Rice Syrup by Lundberg)

1. Preheat oven to 300°F. Oil a 9- by 9- by 2-inch baking pan.
2. In a large bowl, stir together all ingredients except rice syrup.
3. Add rice syrup 1 tablespoon at a time, stirring well after each addition.
4. Pour mixture into prepared baking pan. Dampen hands with water and press mixture firmly into pan.
5. Bake 15 minutes or until bars feel dry and not sticky to the touch.
6. Remove pan from oven and place on a wire rack to cool for 15 to 18 minutes. With a down-up motion, use a spatula to cut into 9 bars. Remove bars from pan and place in an airtight container. Leave in bar shape or break into small pieces to serve as caramel "popcorn." Do not refrigerate.

Yield: 9 bars

PER BAR

Calories: 64
Protein: 0.7 g
Fat: less than 0.1 g
Carbohydrate: 15.5 g

Sodium: 76.3 mg
Diabetic exchanges
  Bread: ½
  Fruit: ½

Rice ''Popcorn''

5 rice cakes, crumbled (use any brand; omit additional salt if using salted rice cakes)

Scant ¼ teaspoon sea salt

Generous ¼ teaspoon allspice

Generous 4 tablespoons rice syrup (Westbrae Natural Brown Rice Syrup)

1. Preheat oven to 300°F. Oil a 9- by 9- by 2-inch baking pan.
2. In a large bowl, stir together all ingredients except rice syrup.
3. Add rice syrup, 1 tablespoon at a time, stirring well after each addition.
4. Pour mixture into prepared baking pan. Dampen hands with water and press mixture firmly into pan.
5. Bake 15 minutes or until mixture feels dry and not sticky to the touch.
6. Remove pan from oven and place on a wire rack to cool for 5 minutes. Use a spatula to cut and break mixture into whatever size pieces are desired. Serve as ''popcorn.'' Do not refrigerate. Store in an airtight container.

Yield: 9 servings

PER SERVING

Calories: 38.2
Protein: 0.6 g
Fat: less than 0.1 g
Carbohydrate: 8.3 g

Sodium: 76.1 mg
Diabetic exchanges
  Bread: ½

COLD
FRESH FRUIT
DRINKS
AND
SORBETS

*n*othing beats the taste of a cold fruit drink or fruit malt or fruit sorbet, especially in the summer. And a bowl of fresh fruit salad can be the perfect finishing touch to any special meal. Almost any fruit or combination of fruits will work. Just remember that for the best taste and appearance and for maximum vitamin content, you should choose fruit that is undamaged and at the height of ripeness.

Because of the many variables, it is difficult to provide useful nutritional analyses for the recipes in this chapter. The following charts should provide some guidance, however.

Nutritional Analysis of Fresh Fruit

Fresh Fruit	Calories	Protein (grams)	Fat (grams)	Carbohydrate (grams)	Sodium (milligrams)	Diabetic Exchanges
Apple (1 medium)	81	0.3	0.5	21.0	1.0	Fruit: 1⅓
Apricot (3 medium)	51	1.5	0.4	11.8	1.0	Fruit: 1
Banana, mashed (per cup)	207	2.3	1.1	52.7	2.0	Fruit: 3½
Blueberries (per cup)	82	1.0	0.6	20.5	9.0	Fruit: 1⅓
Cantaloupe (½ of 5-inch-diameter fruit)	80	2.5	0.7	18.0	23.1	Fruit: 1⅓

Fresh Fruit	Calories	Protein (grams)	Fat (grams)	Carbohydrate (grams)	Sodium (milligrams)	Diabetic Exchanges
Cherries, sweet (20 cherries)	98	1.6	1.3	22.5	0.9	Fruit: 1½
Grapefruit (½ medium)	39	0.8	0.1	9.9	0	Fruit: ½
Grapes (per cup)	114	1.1	0.9	28.4	3.0	Fruit: 2
Honeydew (2- × 7-inch slice)	46	0.6	0.1	11.8	12.9	Fruit: ¾
Kiwi (2 fruit)	92	1.5	0.7	22.6	8.0	Fruit: 1½
Mango (1 medium)	135	1.1	0.6	35.2	3.8	Fruit: 2¼
Nectarine (1 medium)	67	1.3	0.6	16.0	0	Fruit: 1
Orange (1 medium)	62	1.2	0.2	15.4	0	Fruit: 1
Papaya (1 medium)	117	1.9	0.4	29.8	8.0	Fruit: 2
Peach (per cup)	73	1.2	0.2	18.9	1.0	Fruit: 1¼
Pear (1 medium)	98	0.7	0.7	25.1	1.0	Fruit: 1½
Plum (3 medium)	119	1.7	1.4	28.3	0	Fruit: 2
Raspberries (per cup)	61	1.1	0.7	14.2	0	Fruit: 1
Strawberries (per cup)	45	0.9	0.6	10.5	2.0	Fruit: ¾
Watermelon (per cup)	50	1.0	0.7	11.5	3.0	Fruit: ¾

Nutritional Analysis of Fruit Juices

Unsweetened Fruit Juices	Calories	Protein (grams)	Fat (grams)	Carbohydrate (grams)	Sodium (milligrams)	Diabetic Exchanges
Apple (per cup)	116	0.2	0.3	29.0	5.0	Fruit: 2
Apricot nectar (per cup)	120	0.7	0.2	30.0	0	Fruit: 2
Grape (per cup)	155	1.4	0.2	37.9	8.0	Fruit: 2½
Grapefruit (per cup)	96	1.2	0.3	22.7	2.0	Fruit: 1½
Lemon (per tablespoon)	4	0.1	0	1.3	0.1	Free
Orange (per cup)	111	1.7	0.5	25.8	2.0	Fruit: 2
Peach nectar (per cup)	100	0.5	0	25.0	2.0	Fruit: 1⅔
Pear nectar (per cup)	110	0.7	0.5	28.0	2.0	Fruit: 2
Pineapple (per cup)	139	0.8	0.2	34.4	5.0	Fruit: 2¼
Prune (per cup)	181	1.6	0.1	44.6	5.0	Fruit: 3

Nutritional Analysis of Frozen Fruit Juice Concentrates

(All data is for Minute Maid Juices® and is based on 1 cup—8 ounces—of the actual concentrate, unsweetened, and undiluted with water.)

Frozen Fruit Juice Concentrates	Calories	Protein (grams)	Fat (grams)	Carbohydrate (grams)	Sodium (milligrams)	Diabetic Exchanges
Apple	485	0.6	1.1	120.8	121.7	Fruit: 8
Grape	533	2.0	1.0	133.3	111.5	Fruit: 8¾
Grapefruit	422	5.9	1.4	105.2	102.9	Fruit: 7
Orange (Regular, Country Style, Premium Choice, Premium Choice Country Style, and Pulp Free)	485	7.4	0.6	116.6	101.4	Fruit: 8
Orange (Calcium Fortified)	496	7.4	0.6	116.6	101.4	Fruit: 8
Orange (Reduced Acid)	475	7.4	0.6	116.6	101.4	Fruit: 7¾
Pineapple	528	4.0	0.3	129.1	100.8	Fruit: 8½

Fruit Frappe

1 cup unsweetened fruit (peach, pear,
   berries, banana)
4 ice cubes

Place fruit and ice cubes in blender and blend to desired consistency.

Yield: 1 serving

Fruit Soda

½ cup unsweetened fruit juice of choice
   or combination of juices
½ cup sparkling mineral water
Lemon or lime slice (optional)

Combine juice and mineral water. If desired, garnish with lemon or lime.

Yield: 1 serving

Peach Shake

2 cups peeled, pitted, and sliced peaches
¼ cup cold water

Place peaches and water in blender and blend to desired consistency.

Yield: 2 servings

Banana Shake

1 banana, peeled and sliced
1 cup cold water

Place banana and water in blender and blend to desired consistency.

Yield: 1 serving

Fruit Sherbet

1 cup partially thawed frozen fruit

Place fruit in blender or food processor and blend until the fruit is the consistency of sherbet. Serve immediately.

Yield: 1 serving

Orange Sherbet

⅓ cup unsweetened pineapple juice
  concentrate
⅓ cup unsweetened orange juice
  concentrate

¾ cup plus 2 tablespoons water
1 tablespoon olive oil

1. In a medium-sized mixing bowl, combine all ingredients and beat with an electric mixer for 30 seconds every 30 to 45 minutes for a period of 3 to 3½ hours. Between beatings, place mixture in freezer.

2. Ten minutes before serving, remove mixture from freezer. Let it sit for 5 to 10 minutes at room temperature, then beat with mixer for 30 seconds and serve.

Yield: 2 servings

Fresh Fruit Ice Cream

1 frozen banana (to freeze, place
  unpeeled ripe banana in airtight
  plastic bag in freezer)

1 to 2 tablespoons chopped fruit of your
  choice
½ tablespoon chopped nuts (optional)

Remove banana from freezer and thaw for ½ hour. Peel and mash partially thawed banana with a fork. Add chopped fruit and nuts, and stir. Serve immediately.

Yield: 1 serving

Chocolate Ice Cream

4 bananas, peeled
4 squares Baker's All-Natural
   Unsweetened Chocolate
3 tablespoons water

1. In a medium-sized bowl, mash bananas.
2. Melt chocolate with water in top of a double boiler.
3. Add melted chocolate and water to bananas, stir, and freeze before serving.

Yield: 4 servings

Raspberry Popsicles

¼ cup water
10 raspberries (red)
1 peach or nectarine, peeled, pitted, and
   sliced
4 to 5 ice cubes

Place water, fruit, and one ice cube in blender and blend, adding one ice cube at a time, until mixture is the consistency of slush. Pour into plastic molds, adding popsicle sticks if desired, to make real popsicles. Freeze.

Yield: 6 servings

Chocolate Pudding Pops

Prepare Chocolate Pudding (page 111) according to directions. Let cool for 15 minutes, stir, then cool for another 15 minutes. Stir, then spoon mixture into plastic popsicle molds, adding popsicle sticks if desired to make real popsicles. Freeze.

Yield: 8 to 12 servings

Fresh Fruit Bowl

1 banana, peeled, cut in slices, and dipped in orange juice
1 apple, peeled, cored, sliced, and dipped in orange juice
1 orange, peeled and sliced
1 peach, peeled, pitted, sliced, and dipped in orange juice
10 strawberries, hulled and sliced

10 seedless grapes, white and/or red
4 kiwis, peeled and sliced
½ cantaloupe, with rind and seeds removed, cut in slices
¼ honeydew melon, with rind and seeds removed, cut in slices
1 cup watermelon, with rind removed, cut in slices

Combine all fruits in large bowl or in half of a scooped-out watermelon. Refrigerate, covered, until ready to serve.

Yield: 8 servings

INDEX